Don't Be A Stranger

Creating Connections & Memorable First Impressions in Everyday Life

Elicia Nademin, Ph.D., ABPP

Printed in the United States of America

First Printing, 2019

ISBN 978-0-578-60216-5

EliciaN@gmail.com
Scottsdale, AZ 00000

www.4ANewYou2.com

Back Cover image:
Jenn Frieler Kerfeld, Meyer's Photography Studio Inc.

First Edition
14 13 12 11 10 / 10 9 8 7 6 5 4 3 2 1

Dedication

*T*his book is dedicated to my mother, Farideh Nademin, my sweet pup Kaylie, and my beloved late father, Ali Nademin. My father was without question the most incredible man I've ever met, and I especially hope this book may serve as a tribute to his memory. He was kind, gentle, tender-hearted, and a gentleman in all definitions of the word. My father inspired in me a passion for self-development and impacting lives by always teaching me to finish what I start and follow through on my heart's desires. Well, in this case, my heart's desire is to fulfill what was his...to have his daughter publish.

My primary wish in writing this is to preserve and honor the kindness and compassion my father taught me to have for strangers who carry invisible wounds. If I can inspire one more person to do the same for others, I will have left the world a slightly better place than I found it.

This one's for you,
Daddy.

Table of Contents

Table of Contents

Foreword

resident Lincoln was quoted to have said, "In the end, it's not the years in your life but the life in your years" that count most. I couldn't agree more...it would be silly to argue with President Lincoln anyway, don't you think?

The idea for this book came to me three days before I started writing, yet I can't take credit for the spark of genius, and I can call it that since I'm giving credit to someone else. First things first, about seven years ago, I was in the car with my late father. He was in his 80's then and having a 'proud dad' moment, reflecting on my achievements as an up-and-coming Psychologist in Arizona. That day in the car, he caught me off guard. I had finally made it as a Psychologist, completed licensure, and established the foundation for a great career. I was through my doctorate, had my dissertation published, and was finally feeling more settled. I was ready to breathe deeply and enjoy the ride, figuratively and literally, when my father randomly asked me when I'd be writing my book. Never had he nor I mentioned writing a book. I was stunned that he thought there was more to do.

Many of us are guilty of setting goal after goal without stopping to smell the roses (which are incidentally my and my father's favorite flower that he grew over the carport of my childhood home). I teased Daddy that he was ridiculous and that there would be no book-writing for his little girl. After five years of reading graduate school texts, a dissertation, publication of multiple scholarly journal articles, and months of studying for my licensure exam, I didn't think I'd ever *read* another book let alone write one. Well, 'Hello, I'm Elicia, and I'm the author of this book you're reading.' Not only that, I'm proud to be fulfilling my father's wish by writing this book in honor of his beautiful memory.

One of my favorite things in life is talking to strangers, laughing with strangers, and connecting with hearts around the world. It's an ever-present reminder of the random kindness surrounding us. The topic for this book came as randomly as the strangers who come into my life. I've drafted ideas for several books in the past, but each time something (insecurities, competing priorities, fears, etc.) got in the way, and the process didn't flow naturally. Then, something this month clicked. I asked my inner child what would make her soul smile and fuel her inner light so she might glow outward. I asked my buddy Steve W. what he felt I exude naturally that others might be interested in learning about in a quick read book. After several jokes, he blurted out, "why don't you write about connecting with people? You love talking to strangers, and you're the best connector I know!" The flame in me was sparked. Steve W., *consider* this your 15 minutes of fame (or 15 seconds depending on how quickly you read that sentence).

Will you humor me as I share a bit more with you about my father? He was the most incredible man I've met in my life. Much of what I am today and everything I strive still to become are due to the courage, grit, passion, and love he instilled in me. He modeled a gentle manner, integrity, humility, patience, commitment, work ethic, warmth, and grace. He was and remains a pure example of virtues I pursue daily. He is the measuring stick by which I gauge my behavior. Everything I do in my life is done to make him proud…not in an unhealthy, misaligned way but in a sincere "I want to make my father proud of the woman he helped raise" way. I want to honor the beloved man I lost far too soon. My father passed two years later in 2014.

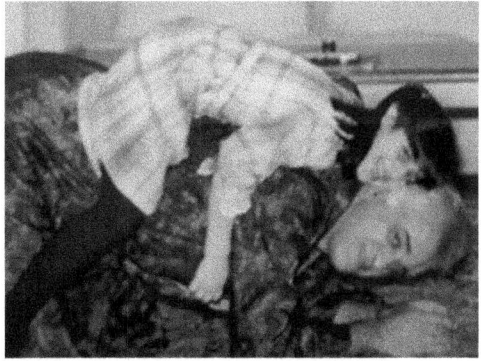

All that said, while some authors are passionate about a topic, I am passionate about fulfilling a dream, a vision, a project through which I could leave a legacy and something of value to others. So, Steve's the inspiration for the book topic, and Karen Casey (2003), author of *Fearless Relationships*, is my inspiration for the structure of the book. Casey's book is an easy read on simple rules for maintaining lifelong contentment in relationships. Each chapter presents skills that foster deeper emotional intimacy in managing oneself in relationships, and I've similarly focused each chapter on specific behaviors for facilitating connections in initial meetings. Sometimes that's where the connection ends, and that's ok. Short-lived meetings are no less meaningful. I've known many momentary connections to have left unforgettable imprints in my life, and I don't believe the Universe makes mistakes. As a board certified psychologist in behavioral and cognitive psychology, I have seen and experienced time and again the impact of changing our patterns of behavior and how we think and talk on our lives and relationships. Thus, each chapter below focuses on different behaviors we can regulate to change our patterns of relating to others and showing up in life.

I've met countless incredible people along my life's journey, and I especially delight in remembering people whose ears I talked off for hours on an airplane as a little girl (*albeit, they may not*). I love recalling plumbers I chatted up while my father paid them to repair things by the hour, friends I've met lounging at a resort pool in Mexico, and patrons I laughed with over music and debauchery at piano bars in major cities. I've made friends enjoying dinners at community Teppanyaki tables in the US and Mexico and while on adventures on tropical excursions. I've connected with fellow dog-lovers at the dog park, had playful exchanges with people in traffic, and enjoyed banter over pumping gas at the gas station. I've made life-long friends volunteering for charity functions and simply sitting at a restaurant or coffee bar near home. Even Diana, one of my dear friends and readers for this book, I met sitting at a local wine bar that was hosting a viewing for fans of the *Bachelor* TV series (please don't judge me, it's my guilty pleasure). William Butler Yeats is credited with having said, "*Strangers are "friends you haven't met yet."* I couldn't agree more. Let's create a new relationship with the word *stranger*.

I've always taken for granted how easy it's been for me to establish random connections because it has come so naturally for so long, but it didn't always, and I realize it doesn't for everyone. I've delineated my "how-to" approach to help others realize how much control they have in creating rich and meaningful new connections in their own lives. If I could learn, why couldn't you?

Sometimes you connect with someone you'll never see again but with whom you'll share deep, meaningful conversations about life and love. Other times, you'll return from random networking events, dinners, or trips with lifelong friendships. I believe you're meant to be right where you are at any given moment in time to learn lessons you may not know you're set up for.

What if you lived life considering that everyone you meet is perfectly enlightened and here to teach you something? Perhaps the obnoxious driver or disrespectful teenager is here to teach you virtues of grace and patience. What if the elderly couple walking slowly in front of you while you grab groceries rushed on your way home from work is a reminder of patience and the finiteness of time and life? What if you treated each moment with curiosity or as an adventure, an adventure that will reveal a moral? How different would your connections and relationships feel if you asked for clarification, rather than assuming intentions, thoughts, or feelings that are not fact? What if you task yourself to uncover what lesson the people in your life are here to teach you? Are you willing and humble enough to let them?

With all the self-help books written over the years, you'd think we'd all be experts at creating healthy, happy, lasting relationships with stellar communication. Not to mention, as a psychologist, I'm expected to be impeccable at managing relationships. Well, I am a content expert...now, if only life were a textbook and I were the author of every interaction...but, it's not and I'm not. Relationships involve two or more dynamic people with varying degrees of emotional and life experience that color and skew neutrality. I can manage and navigate relationships, quite well actually, but that doesn't mean they're always fulfilling, that I always get what I want, or that I always apply what I know.

It's challenging, exhausting, and unrealistic to be held to a standard of emotional, social, and professional perfection, so let's let that go, and simply talk about what small skills can help you foster more successful, feel-good connections with strangers. Trust that you will fall short in many opportunities, especially as you first start practicing. Challenge yourself to reflect and learn from each scenario. We tend to learn more from failed opportunities than from successes. I've failed many times at making and maintaining connections, but I remind myself that I am 100% accountable to myself. If it went well, I ask how I helped that along. If it went poorly, I ask how I got in my own way. Perhaps I was in my head or letting my mood interfere with my facial expression, tone of voice, or greeting. None of the techniques laid out in this book are foolproof. Try what you're willing, challenge yourself out of your comfort zone, and assess what feels in alignment with who you are. *Practice makes progress, not perfection.* Be true to yourself...but be careful. Sometimes what *"feels" true* to you is keeping you 'small.' *The true you is capable of far more than you give yourself credit for.* You may inadvertently be playing it safe to avoid stepping out of your emotional comfort zone for fear of judgment, rejection, or failure. Insecurity and fear have great ways of masking themselves as "I don't wanna" and "That's not me."

Please keep in mind reading all the literature in the world isn't enough to make any of us experts at all relationships. Why didn't Andre Agassi's coach win all the tennis tournaments? If all it took was knowledge, he might have. Paying for a gym membership and reading books on fitness alone won't get you tone. You've got to do the exercises and use the equipment *consistently, safely, and effectively* to see results *over time.* When it comes to talking to strangers, your tools are your emotional, relational, verbal, and nonverbal skills as laid out in this book. Knowledge alone isn't enough. *Applying knowledge* while *managing yourself* is critical to success in life and relationships. *Are you prepared to evolve?*

With that, let's move forward.

Chapter 1:
To Whom This May Concern

*W*hoever said relationships are easy L-I-E-D through their teeth. First, you've got to get through an initial meeting that ignites enough mutual curiosity to warrant further pursuit. If there is initial intrigue in developing a relationship, you'll want to consider how best to balance time, intentions, and a follow-up plan so the connection grows roots. If you don't want to further the connection, you'll want to consider how to politely extricate yourself from further engaging. In deciding which way to go, you may consider a host of questions. Is this connection with someone you'd enjoy talking to again? Would the relationship be for personal or professional reasons? Would it be self-serving, or would it feel mutual? Is this someone you can trust? Is this person good, kind, and genuine? Does the other person reciprocate interest? It can be quite exhausting. Then again, not everyone puts so much thought into initial meetings. Some people rely only on an inherent "feeling" that can be enlightened...or misleading.

At its core, this book is about talking to strangers and making memorable first impressions in everyday life, from the grocery store, out-of-town resort, or other casual venues to more formal networking, conferences, or job interviews. Please know, I'm referring to strangers perceived to be safe and met in safe settings. I'm asking you to trust your intuition on this or consult other books, guardians, or guidance on differentiating between safe and unsafe strangers.

Talking to strangers is one of my favorite activities in life! You don't hear that often, and yet doing so is one of the quickest ways to see your impact on the world. It's also the scariest for many because it tends to trigger people's inherent fears of rejection. This book is not only to share my passion for people but also to help anyone wanting to hone their skills for fostering more memorable first impressions, connecting with strangers, and identifying whether and how to build relationships from there. Not every connection is destined or healthy to build on. Whether for networking, friendship, romance, or in starting a new job, first impressions are critical to whether relationships get off the ground.

Connecting with strangers sparks my inner light. This book is my attempt to offer a roadmap of how I approach chance meetings in hopes that others may feel more confident doing so. Many brief encounters in my life have transitioned into deep friendship or business partnership. May you live life excited to learn who you'll meet and what the Universe may intend for that meeting.

Introverts may be cringing at the idea of talking to strangers, but I find that introverts are quite adept at cultivating highly meaningful connections and relationships! I might even argue introverts have greater bandwidth for depth in their relationships as they seem to develop deep bonds with fewer people among whom they spread their attention. The suggestions I offer can be applied in part to connections made online, in small venues, one-on-one interactions, and less socially stimulating environments as well. I do believe you'll get the most benefit out of trying these skills in in-person settings though.

Who is this book NOT for? This book is not for people who want to learn tools for manipulating others for personal gain. It is also *not* for *unsafe* strangers who might do harm. This might seem silly to say, but I wouldn't have forgiven myself if I didn't state the obvious. Please check your intentions.

It may be tempting to assume these techniques don't work if they don't work right away, or if they don't work consistently each time. Humans are unpredictable creatures with unique temperaments and histories. Refrain from blaming or shaming, and instead show curiosity for others as you embark on the adventure of talking to strangers. Doing so will prepare you to relate more positively to them. Ruiz (2012) said in his globally renowned text *The Four Agreements* that another person's behavior is "never about you." Remembering this will make it easier to not internalize how others in a room may (or may not) interact with you *when you are presenting as your best self.* Let's face it, the truth is if you present rudely, loudly, arrogantly, or any other *-ly* word that is traditionally received poorly, other people's reactions *might be* about you. Focus on communicating confidence, manner, and warmth. People may still bring 'their stuff' to the interaction, but the more compassion you show others, the more difficult it will be for them to respond negatively to you.

Before moving forward, please keep a journal handy to record some of your favorite memories of connecting with new people. Perhaps the people you write about are still in your life, perhaps not. They're unforgettable, nonetheless. What made the interactions special or different than your usual encounters? What went well and how did you present initially? What did you wear? How and where were you standing or sitting? Who started the conversation, and what was said? What did you not say? Keep notes on how, when, and where you might apply each skill I present differently than how you've done in the past.

Authentic, healthy relationships are mutually satisfying ones wherein both parties benefit from the union, short-term or otherwise. One of my favorite memories was in connecting with three lovely women while gleefully riding camels beachfront in Cabo. We still keep in touch from time to time and I always think of them and smile when I see a camel. Regardless of how you meet someone, reciprocity is important. This text is intended as

somewhat of a reference manual for fostering genuine, memorable connections. Each person matters for whatever moment in time you co-exist.

A note of caution before you proceed: *If you are in a romantic relationship while developing the skills laid out in this book, please let your partner know in advance of your plans to practice talking to strangers. This is to avoid confusion or misinterpretation of intentions later.* You might even try these exercises with your partner and ask one another for feedback on how you present.

Aristotle's words[1] have been interpreted to propose: "We are what we repeatedly do. Excellence, then, is not an act, but a habit." Aristotle's original writings cite achieving "moral excellence" (sometimes translated as "virtue") through good habits. In Book II of Aristotle's "Nicomachean Ethics" based on lectures he gave in Athens in the fourth century BCE, Aristotle was quoted: "Excellence, then, being of these two kinds, intellectual and moral, intellectual excellence owes its birth and growth mainly to instruction, and so requires time and experience, while moral excellence is the result of habit or custom."

With that, let's start repeating.

---

[1] www.CheckYourFact.com supports that while reminiscent of Aristotelian thought, this quote is often misattributed to Aristotle and is in fact an interpretation of his words by Will Durant, having originated in the 1926 book, "The Story of Philosophy." Durant chronicled works of history's great philosophers, including Aristotle, and in essence, captured the sentiments of Aristotle more succinctly and in his own words.

Chapter 2:

First Impressions

J ournalist and best-selling author in Social Psychology Malcolm Gladwell explains in his book *Blink: The Power of Thinking Without Thinking* (2005) that first impressions are often made instantaneously. He proposes that people "thin-slice" whenever they encounter a new person or situation or "have to make sense of something quickly." Thin-slicing refers to the ability to find patterns in events based on narrow windows of experience. Gladwell describes snap judgments as "enormously quick" and "unconscious," relying on "the thinnest slices of experience." This isn't because people are judgmental, unkind or wanting to stereotype but because we live in a fast-paced culture with co-occurring influences. Our brains want to quickly compartmentalize which relationships feel emotionally or professionally 'safe.' The problem, of course, lies in that when people thin-slice, they do so not from fact but from personal experience, informed by their beliefs, attitudes, values, bias, and education. This book is meant to help you create fertile ground to increase your chances of attracting more positive interactions in light of this.

Gladwell cautions that while helpful, thin-slicing can also have great implications for decision-making around hiring practices, friendship, business collaborations, and more. How often have you said, "I don't care what people think." Well, would you care if you knew that your future *could* depend on it? After all, you could miss out on that job, a friendship, a relationship or simply a wonderful memory if you leave someone with a negative impression. The tendency to make snap judgments is not necessarily a bad thing so expecting others to change is unwise, unhealthy, and unhelpful. Instead, accept that humans have evolved in their abilities to immediately assess safety in their environments by making quick judgment calls upon meeting others for a multitude of valid reasons, including predicting the future health of a relationship. We wouldn't want to discourage this skill any more than we wouldn't want to eliminate intuition. Thus, release others of expectations of change, and change yourself. You, alone, are the only person whose behaviors and reactions you can predict and control.

It is very hard to rewrite a poor first impression. Throughout this book, I'll be asking that you consider authentically modifying the *you* you present to the world. Change *how* you show up by managing what you say and do differently. I'm not asking you to fake *you*. I am asking you to 'fake *it* till you make it.' Faking *it* is about changing your patterns and impression management, *not* to be manipulative but to practice new and healthier habits that attract more positive interactions with others. I can't guarantee how others will respond to you but can say with confidence that doing so will increase the likelihood that more people will respond to you positively and that you'll enjoy your interactions more. I am asking that you proceed with blind faith that people will see you differently as you teach yourself to show up differently.

If you're someone who says, "no one ever approaches me," I challenge you to ask yourself what energy or nonverbal cues you give off. I have found no scarcity of people in my world to connect with. I have, however, found a scarcity of approachable energy. I've found the people who complain about seldom getting approached are usually less approachable.

As *you* change and show up as friendlier, more inviting, and safer, others will respond to you differently.

What do I mean by safe? Many people fear rejection. Sometimes the most arrogant person in a room has deep underlying insecurities. If you present yourself in a way that appears warm and welcoming, you are less likely to meet others' defenses and more likely to have positive, memorable interactions in the moments you create.

Have you noticed that some people choose to put their best foot forward only if they feel there's something to gain in the interaction? I'd like to propose you put your best foot forward in assuming every new encounter is a gift. *Choose* to treat everyone with respect. Practice positively engaging everyone, not because a person deserves it or the event demands it but because you choose to carry yourself as such. Do so whether you feel well or not, whether you think you're compatible or not, whether they talk a certain way or not, and whether they're dressed a certain way or not. Create a consistent pattern of behaviors over time and diverse scenarios, and be curious, not critical.

When first impressions are negative, they may be based on poor social skills or defense mechanisms like arrogance, fear, withdrawal, talking too much or not enough, or lack of polish that leaves others questioning compatibility, confidence, or warmth. We're not going to change the world in one conversation, but we can change the possible course of a relationship by reserving judgment and giving everyone the benefit of the doubt. Treat all with kindness, warmth, and respect. How you present will leave people with more or less interest in getting to know you. You can leave people recalling your interaction positively or wishing to forget it. Or, you might simply leave no imprint at all. Which would you prefer?

I sometimes have people in my life feel they can't relate to me because they believe talking to strangers comes easily to me. It may feel natural now, but it didn't always. Don't get me wrong. I've always loved interactions with strangers. I loved talking to people who were within an arm's reach and who sparked a conversation with me (hence, the plumber, a server, electrician, neighbors on airplanes who politely yet naively said hello not realizing what they were getting themselves into for the next few hours). Notice, these were mostly people paid or otherwise obliged to be nice to me, so they seemed 'safer.' My life changed most dramatically when I took control and began going out of my way to cultivate more memories and conversations with strangers.

Few who know me today believe I grew up painfully shy. In my youth, I was afraid of what others would think of me if I said or did something foolish. I seldom went anywhere alone. I avoided walking up to people or chatting them up if I did. I was the child hiding behind my mom. I took hours to warm up to the same group of friends at family events each weekend. I was the person who'd look for the first place to sit when entering a crowded room, wanting to shrink and be anything *but* noticed. It's hard to even remember myself that way. You can imagine these patterns didn't leave me making great first impressions let alone lasting ones. I never felt like I fit in, everyone always seemed 'cooler' 'smoother,' and 'funner' (yes, I made that up). As a budding adult going through graduate school and work, I started to find my voice. I've evolved into the *me* people know today, as I've made doing so fun.

How I owned my power in creating first impressions changed in 2008 when a friend from elementary school invited me to a concert. The concert was loud, crowded, and upbeat. Everyone was waving their arms and jumping around with joy. I was in awe. I loved it and was breathing it in. I was stunned when my friend leaned in and asked if I was bored. He assumed I wasn't having a good time because I wasn't smiling. I had RBF and didn't know it! For those who don't know what RBF stands for, it's *Resting Bitch Face*! Forgive the language, but it's a very real thing that men and women alike suffer from.

RBF is commonly defined as a facial expression that unintentionally (or intentionally) appears displeased, unfriendly, annoyed, bored, frustrated, angry, or another negative feeling, even when a person is simply feeling relaxed, neutral, or contemplative. I had NO idea my face *lived* there when I felt nervous, shy, or simply out of my element. The funny thing is that my face now is anything but that most days. My face now is one of the most expressive faces I know, but I had to train it to be that way. When I teach medical students, I instruct them to reflect on their resting facial expressions and to rule out RBF because of the impact it can have on patient care. Whether patients feel liked by their provider affects whether they return for treatment and comply with recommendations. Thus, training facial expressions to be inviting and pleasant can be career-altering (and life-altering). I encourage students to ask family/friends for feedback on how they present, and I ask the same of you. I suggest giving permission that whoever you ask deliver feedback honestly yet respectfully and constructively with suggestions for how you present in first impressions. Also ask their opinion on slight tweaks, like altering of eye contact, a head nod, or a smile that they believe might make a difference in how you present. *Caution, please use judgment in who you ask. I don't recommend you ask a person known to be caustic, critical, or hurtful. Ask someone who might give feedback in a kind, productive manner.*

I can imagine readers might have a knee jerk reaction and say, "Live, and let live. That's just my face." But, if you knew your face might constantly rob you of positive attention and life experiences and a simple smile, raise of your eyebrows, or slight modification in mouth movements practiced over time could significantly change the trajectory of your relationships, would you feel differently? I certainly did. My life completely changed after that concert.

My *choice* to smile and to show more engagement nonverbally has impacted not only others' experiences of me but ultimately my own overall experience of myself. I feel powerful. Even faking a smile improves my overall mood in just minutes and changes how others respond to me. I now delight in watching how the world around me changes in response to subtle changes I make in my facial expressions. In fact, I can usually predict the type of experience I'll have at a function or new experience based on the facial expression I have *walking in*to it. It took mindful attention to nonverbal signs, practice over many situations over time, and strength of character to continue to practice even (*and especially*) when I didn't want to. Practicing these skills when I didn't feel like it led to my feeling like it. Learn more on how to address RBF in Chapter 6 on Bringing the Light by *smiling*.

The suggestions herein are not necessarily based on scientific research but on results of my personal lived experience and that of countless patients and friends. The first impression is made up of an integration of skills laid out in this book that together form the memory others are left with. Practicing these skills over time can override fears and insecurities, helping you present vulnerably as your best self. I'd argue our best *self* tends to emerge in moments of joy, so I propose creating more of those. Find things to laugh about with strangers. Accentuate attention to manners, grace, pleasant demeanor, humility, and positivity that create space for others to present their best selves as well.

I believe what often sets people apart in their ability to make strong connections is their skill in fostering positive first impressions. The strength and reliability of follow-up are also important if a relationship is to continue, but initial impressions and greetings are critical. How are you with eye contact? Do you interrupt when in dialogue or talk over others? What does your tone of voice sound like? Do you inflect up or down? Do you shy away from sharing your opinion for fear of what others might say or think? Do you sit/stand alone and wait for others to come to you? Are your thoughts positive or negative about the people and circumstances around you? Do you pass judgment and make global assumptions about people based on a few things they say? Are you quick to minimize others' achievements? Are you focused on how you're feeling, or do you think of others? Are you lost in thought about the "best, wittiest, most thoughtful thing to say?" Do you exchange contact information to facilitate follow-up? Do you take responsibility for then doing so, letting the person you met know you appreciated the shared meeting and found that moment in time to be memorable? I'll bring many of these up in the chapters that follow with tips on how to overcome barriers in each area.

In any situation, I urge you to remain focused on being the light and finding the light in a room. What do I mean by this? Have you ever seen a firefly in real life? I grew up in Washington, D.C., and fireflies[2] are one of my favorite memories from childhood, which is ironic because I'm very squeamish about insects. In the darkest of skies, though, all of a sudden, beautiful glowing mini-orbs would momentarily appear then fade, only to skip around playfully and re-appear somewhere else. I'd find myself running around giggling and chasing the beautiful lights that seemed blissfully to be teasing me. I'm not suggesting you fade out. I am suggesting you be that light others are curiously and excitedly drawn to and want to frolic around with! We don't frolic enough in today's world, and so long as you're breathing it's not too late to start. My average therapy patient is over 70 years old, so I'm the last person to tell that you're "too old to change."

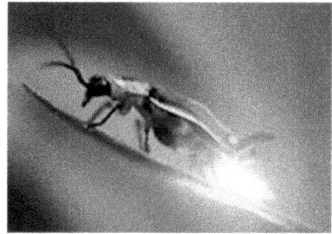

I believe part of the beauty in this journey of life is that everyone has a light. Make it an adventure to find yours, and let others know that you see theirs. This is another way of simply saying 'bring out the best in others,' and help them shine! I'm not suggesting you take responsibility for others but that you *help* create an environment that helps disarm others' defenses.

---

[2] Photo #71142 titled "The Surfer," taken of species Photinus Piralis by Radim Schreiber. Available at www.FireflyExperience.com.

This helps them feel more comfortable and likely to express themselves around you.

Networking and talking to strangers are less about what you say and more about how you say it, the feeling you leave people with, and the energy you emanate. Maya Angelou's quote comes to mind: *"I've learned that people will forget what you said, people will forget what you did, but people will never forget how you made them feel."* I live life by this premise. My favorite memories are fuzzy in details but profound in the depth of the connection shared. I remember feelings of joy and of my heart skipping a beat. I remember how deeply I've laughed and when someone brought me to giggles even if I don't remember how.

Specific to attitude, please be honest with yourself and recognize you may be unconsciously creating the very negative experience you want to avoid by expecting discomfort where you go. There's a great metaphor on withholding expectations in the book *Bring Me the Rhinoceros*. The author asks readers to predict the next item in the sequence: "2-4-6-..." (Tarrant, 2008). What would you assume would come next? Most would say 8...2-4-6-8. The author of this clever book, however, proposes *what if reality were "2-4-6-Rhinosaurus?"* What if reality were *so* different and more exciting than your expectations, but you miss it because your focus is on the wrong *next item* in the sequence? A unique, unimaginable life might be happening while you're looking for the eight! Imagine being like the turtle that rolls over on its back, stares at the sky, and shouts happily, *"Oh my gosh, I'm flying!"* How different would we feel if we saw life with such naive glee? Be that positive person who walks in curiously looking for fireflies in the room instead of the person commenting on what's wrong or missing.

Please welcome a trusted friend or family member to give honest feedback as you adapt these skills. Ask how they feel you present now, especially in initial interactions, and what they notice as you begin to change. Notice how you are received by others. Give explicit permission that they speak openly without fear of defensiveness or punishment. Again, please only ask people likely to respond kindly and constructively.

It is imperative you honestly assess how your current presentation may be contributing to the outcomes you're getting. You may have no idea you're perpetuating the very experiences you don't like. It's like trying to get a fish to discover the water it's swimming in. The water is so fundamental to the way of life of a fish. The fish doesn't understand it's wet. The fish is so immersed in the water it doesn't notice or question the water's existence. Similarly, you may be so immersed in your own ways of *being* and patterns of relating to others you may not realize you're creating the very experiences you don't like. Let's pay attention to the water and make some fun waves. (Thanks to my friend and fellow Psychologist Dr. Frederick S. Wechsler for the fabulous fish analogy). Remember, if you're 100% accountable for what you get, what will you change to get a different result?

Ready? *Meet me inside.*

Chapter 3:
Face Your Fears

*H*ave you ever considered how often you form judgments before you even walk into a room? How often do you assume you "won't meet anyone," that "it'll be a bore," or that "everyone's just there for their own agendas...to push their business...to be seen..." Perhaps you've thought, "I'm not cut out for small talk," or "I hate networking events" (I'm guilty of these). Any idea why we say these things to ourselves or how these thoughts may likely affect the outcome of our experiences? We tend to pass judgments like these and 'foreshadow' the future to protect ourselves from fear; fear of rejection, fear of embarrassment or failure, fear of discomfort. You may fear feeling like the 'uncool' one in the room. Perhaps you have *imposter syndrome*. This is a common fear among high achievers that you're not actually good enough or qualified for what you earned, that someone will one day figure you out and rescind your credentials. It's vital to understand more about our fears so we can address them. Self-awareness is a gift. There's no shame in caring about what others think. Vulnerability, warmth, and shared experience are crucial in connections. As we understand and accept more about ourselves, we are better able to extend compassion while establishing healthy boundaries.

Despite human instincts to want connection, our natural defenses to avoid fears are strong. I'd argue it's instinctive to want to avoid fear. Fear of rejection is profound and often automatic. Sometimes fear manifests as arrogance, entitlement, or avoidance of new or social situations altogether. Other times it shows up as attending an event but missing opportunities to create connections either by cowering, engaging awkwardly, coming on too strongly, joking inappropriately, or overshadowing others in a way that drives them to disengage. Instincts often kick in, and we react. To change, we must remain emotionally present and aware of our self-talk, or the things we think and say to ourselves. *Program positive messages into your mind about whatever experience you want to achieve.* I'm not suggesting you be *fakely* bubbly and happy all the time. If you're having a bad day and want to embrace pain and sadness, do so in ways that may be nurturing and not damaging. Stay home, light candles, nourish yourself with self-care, journal, or watch a favorite show after letting your inner voice and wisdom come through. Or, if you choose to go out, explicitly give yourself permission to *not* meet anyone...to let it be ok to silently look for the beauty around you. Remind yourself that *not* meeting people was your goal if you leave feeling disappointed in not having met people. Keep in mind though you're likely to attract whatever intention, energy, and self-talk you take into the room.

Not only do people generally see what they expect to see, but they often remember what they expect to remember. Our memories are not pure replicas of our past. They are re-creations of it. Our interpretations of memories are what we recall. We make sense of a scene and that interpretation colors what we recall about it. We may settle for distortions of reality when we make negative assumptions based on experience. Each time you walk into an interaction thinking "this is going to be awful/boring," that's what you'll likely get out of it. Be open to a different outcome. If you look for the same 'ole outcome, you might miss something else wonderful.

Imagine everyone you build relationships with is your mirror. What are they reflecting back? Do you like it? Hate it? What about them do you react strongest to? These mirrors are priceless. Listen to what they're here to teach you about what you like or dislike about yourself. Create an image of your *ideal self,* starting with a vision of who you want to be. Think of an actor/actress, family member, or friend you admire. Ask yourself, "What would he/she do in the situation like the one I'm entering?" Your vision is the fundamental driver of change. Start taking steps toward it. *Act as if* you're the person who inspires you.

In the book *The Happiness Makeover (2005),* people are universally said to want happiness. Sometimes their way of pursuing happiness gets in the way of another's. While frustrating, this is not necessarily intentional or hostile. Remind yourself if put off by someone you meet, *'this person is simply trying to be happy and isn't aware of his/her effect on me. I wish them well.'* It's not necessarily a rejection. That person doesn't know you anyway. We don't know the invisible wounds others are carrying. Let's commit to not deepening those injuries and leave a positive imprint on anyone we encounter whenever possible.

I can't say enough about avoiding expectations and challenging prejudgments. Intuition is a powerful, pervasive force. Yet, when expectations are based on fear or assumptions, you'll be distracted by misleading, negative messages you may mistake for intuition. Take two minutes and try something for me, please. Go to the following website and count how many times the players wearing white passed the ball: **https://bit.ly/1bYRDzj** (sorry for the awkward link. If it doesn't work, search YouTube for the under 2-minute video of a co-ed group playing basketball titled, "Selective Attention Test." Please don't turn the page until you do this. *How many passes do you count?*

What did you see? Did you see the unexpected? When participants in these studies knew what to look for, they consistently saw it. Those who didn't were often victim to their bias (and likely yours). Their selective and faulty expectation led to inattentional blindness (Simons & Chabris, 2009). You likely didn't you see it because I set a faulty expectation to prove my point. I told you what to look for, so you looked for that and probably missed the very obvious cue right under your nose. So, if you're looking for *it* (whatever *it* is), you might miss something.

For the next few days, try an exercise from the Carlson (1997) book, *Don't Sweat the Small Stuff, and It's All Small Stuff:* Try a day without expectations. *Don't* expect people to be friendly or considerate. When they're not, you won't be disappointed. *Don't* expect a problem-free day. When problems come up, remind yourself it's simply another hurdle to overcome. Don't expect the opposite; that's still an expectation. Simply be curious and open. Does life feel more graceful as you show curiosity instead of expecting that others *be* a certain way?

Acknowledging a fear of rejection can feel so stigmatized in our culture that it may operate below conscious awareness, like an invisible weapon. Societal messages tend to deem it unattractive to openly admit fear. Think about the military. Fear of being injured, physically or emotionally, can not only distract from the mission at hand but can also result in a clinical syndrome of post-traumatic stress, oversimplified as fears related to reminders of perceived dangers of the past. Many veterans returning from deployment today are trained to prepare for IEDs, underground bombs that might go off at any time without signal or warning. The source of danger may seem absent to the naked eye, yet the fear is very real and can persist for years after service despite return to civilian life. This can create a perpetual state of anxiety, which comes in many shapes and sizes. Fear can be confusingly masked in how we relate to others.

Fear of embarrassment and rejection can feel highly wounding and may also be related to past experiences that affected a sense of self-worth and belonging. When I meet strangers or enter unfamiliar events, I remind myself I can't see others' wounds. I extend grace and compassion, often moreso when I meet people who struggle to hold eye contact. I wonder how I might engage them and even for a moment show them that I *see* them and value their presence. *Be like that.*

Before moving on, let's make something very clear. Fears are great liars. They come up with stories to keep you from evolving and overcoming them. Did you know fear is perpetuated and kept alive by avoidance of the source of fear? The more often you avoid your fear, the more you feed it. It's like sending a message to the brain that says, "Phew!!! Thank goodness you protected me from that awful dangerous situation! I could have died!! Since I listened to you and avoided it, now I'm safe…but only for now. I'll be sure to avoid it again next time since I now know what I'm looking for!"

The best way to overcome fear is to confront it and to confront it time and again. Afraid to talk to strangers? Ok, talk to more of them! Get comfortable being uncomfortable. When I started my skincare business as a Rodan + Fields Independent Consultant, I was in foreign territory. Nothing in life had pushed me out of my comfort zone like owning a business, let alone in sales. What was a successful Psychologist doing selling skincare! I felt like a fish out of water. I was afraid of people's judgment. I was afraid of failure. I found success by following a philosophy I developed: *"Do It Scared, Do It Ugly, Do It Often."* Doing it *scared* goes without saying. I went up to strangers, I went to the networking events, I went out by myself, I traveled alone, and I challenged myself to talk to people everywhere I went even though I felt scared and out of place. Doing it *ugly* meant I expected to embarrass myself. I expected to stumble over my words. I have made awkwardly intense eye contact before. I have felt stuck in moments of silence that went on too long. I kept practicing anyway. I did it *often*…over and over and over again. *And*, I lived to tell you the tale. Little did I know, my passion for talking to strangers would serve me well in immeasurable ways!

In a chapter on fears, I would be remiss not to mention that the reality is some people will judge you. Some people might snicker about you across a room, and you might well just notice. Some people might dislike you for any host of reasons we might only speculate. I once went to a seminar where I was reminded: "Do *not* dim your light for fear of making others uncomfortable with your glow." *Shine proudly*.

I still feel uncomfortable at times. I still feel awkward at times. I do it anyway. I still get scared sometimes. That inner critic still threatens me and tells me 'no one cares' or 'it won't matter.' I do it anyway. I smile anyway. I make eye contact anyway. I present my best self anyway. I show curiosity anyway...you get my drift. When I don't have it in me to be these things, 1 of 2 things happens: 1) I don't have as much fun, and I don't meet as many strangers. I do find, though, that I'm sometimes lucky enough to be somewhere feeling crummy, and there's someone there like me. Despite my mood or output, they engage me. They help bring out the best in me, and it's like the Universe saying: "I've got your back Elicia!" 2) I choose to stay home and nurture my soul in silence, and that's ok too. I will add, I'll almost never cancel plans that are already confirmed. My word is priceless to me. I don't say "maybe," I'm careful not to overcommit, and I have no problem leaving early if my energy simply isn't authentically engaging.

There's a variation of a fable my mother shared with me that I love:

A young boy and his father are riding through town together on a donkey one hot summer day. They have quite a distance to travel. As they go through the first town, they overhear the townsfolk whispering: "What a disgraceful pair. Look at them. Two healthy men atop that poor, tired donkey in this heat! Have they no thought about the donkey's health? Shame on them." Feeling badly, the father dismounts the donkey, allowing his son to ride alone to relieve much of the weight from the donkey's back. In the next town, they overhear the townsfolk whispering again, this time: "Ugh, look at that boy. What a disgrace! The virile young boy atop such a strong donkey while the poor elderly father is left to walk miles in this heat. What if he has a heart attack or suffers heat exhaustion? That young boy should be ashamed!" Oh dear, they didn't want the young boy to be under such verbal attack, so in the following town, the young boy and his father switched places. As you might guess, the townsfolk whispered, "What a disgrace! How can that selfish father allow himself to ride atop that donkey while his son is left to walk alongside them? Look at his frail body! They should be ashamed!" Finally, in the next town over, both father and son dismount the donkey and all three walk together through town, and what did the townsfolk say this time? "Look at that pair of idiots! Two men walking alongside a donkey."[3]

Moral of the story: People will always have an opinion of you no matter what you say or do, so be your best self...not the self that wants to prove something, but your vulnerable self when the walls come down and you welcome in joy...joy for the most memorable moments in life. Some people confuse being themselves with being overly casual in their presentation,

---

[3] Incidentally, in researching the background of this tale, I came across a similar fable entitled *The Man, the Boy, and the Donkey* in Æsop. (Sixth century B.C.) Fables in The Harvard Classics. The donkey dies in the end and that was an awful ending, so I like my mother's version better. Additional versions may be found in Mediaeval collections and other classification systems for folklore narratives, such as Aarne-Thompson.

attire, manner, or speech. I would argue when making a first impression, be the self you'd want to be remembered as, not a renegade but the self who takes pride in helping others feel at ease.

No matter how good you get at practicing new tools, you won't win over everyone. You won't even win over most, but you'll experience some extraordinary moments along the way. There are a few things to be mindful of in putting yourself out there to connect with more people. 1) You're likely to encounter more unpleasant people. This does not mean people are mostly bad. It means you're bold and courageous in putting yourself out there more than the average person, thus attracting more people into your aura. This will include incredible people you wouldn't have met otherwise but also a few that don't resonate because your reach is so much wider. Pay close attention to your core values. Show curiosity in getting to know others. Withhold judgment and assumptions. Show wisdom in identifying where each connection might best fit in your life's trajectory. Just because people enter your aura doesn't mean they belong there long-term. 2) Other people's reactions to you are not necessarily about you and they're not your business. Maybe they're having a bad day, relationship difficulties, financial or housing issues, medical stressors, etc. Give them the benefit of the doubt, be kind, and assume positive intentions. And if it might be about you, honestly ask yourself why. Perhaps you stumbled and came across as awkward, intense, or withdrawn? Learn more about strategies for developing your new skills in Chapter 4 on Being Ninja-esque.

Carnegie (1981) said in his world-famous text *How to Win Friends and Influence People* that any fool can criticize, condemn, and complain—and most fools do. He goes on to say it takes character and self-control to be understanding, compassionate, and forgiving. Indeed, it is easier to find fault than praise. Carnegie shared the story of John Wanamaker of Wanamaker stores who once said, "It is foolish to scold. I have enough trouble overcoming my own limitations without fretting over the fact that

God has not seen fit to distribute evenly the gift of intelligence." Criticism will only evoke defensiveness and rationalization. Seek to be humble. Let go of the urge to share your wisdom of another's wrong or to 'know better.' Consider what Carnegie shared of Mrs. Mary Todd Lincoln, wife of one of our nation's most influential and loved Presidents. When Mrs. Lincoln and others spoke ill of southerners, Abraham Lincoln replied, "Don't criticize them; they are just what we would be under similar circumstances." Everyone's going through life trying to be happy, and sometimes their happy might get in the way of yours. Wish them well as they continue to skip along blindly to joy.

You will mess up. You will feel like you 'failed' a social opportunity or missed a chance to meet the greatest stranger of your life. I promise you, there are plenty of other opportunities. Simply tell yourself, "Ok, I messed that up. It was awkward but it's ok. I'll do better next time." Avoiding mistakes will only arrest your development. Natural evolution occurs over a sequence of mistakes that result in growth over time. Ask yourself what you learned about each situation so you can challenge yourself to do it differently next time.

Trust yourself to handle difficult news and situations as they emerge rather than worrying about how you *might* handle them *if* they arise. Stop worrying about the hypothetical situations that have not yet arisen. As stated by Allen Saunders, "Life is what's happening while we're busy making other plans[4]."

Much of our anxiety and inner struggle as adults stem from our overactive minds always yearning for the next thing to focus on. While we're eating dinner, we wonder what's for dessert. While we're at a party, we wonder what we'll do tomorrow. *Be present.*

---

[4] According to the _Yale Book of Quotations_ editor Fred R. Shapiro, this quote is attributed to writer and cartoonist Allen Saunders. A variation of the quote, "Life is what happens to us while we are making other plans," was published in Reader's Digest in January 1957.

Mark Twain once said, "I have been through some terrible things in my life, *some of which actually happened.*" The humor and irony speak to the reality of how much time we spend worrying about things that don't happen. Trust yourself to handle criticism or challenge as either comes and at a time when you're able to do so with sound mind. Speak when you have something to say worth listening to. Trust yourself to be stronger, bolder, and more successful than you give yourself credit for.

Jon Kabat-Zinn (1994) said, "wherever you go, there you are." You're meant to be where you are at this exact moment in time. The Universe makes no mistakes. Welcome the discomfort that accompanies new experiences, concentrate, and breathe through it. In doing so, you'll find you not only enjoy things more, but you'll be better at them. As Carlson (1997) proposed, practice being in the eye of the storm—the calm, serene center amidst frenzy and chaos—breathe, listen, let others speak and be right, focus on what you have rather than what you want, and enjoy the glory.

When feeling nervous or pessimistic, I draw strength by recalling the poem, *Our Deepest Fear*[5], authored by motivational speaker and author Marianne Williamson, featured in the film *Coach Carter*. In this poem, Williamson references our deepest fear not of being inadequate but rather of being powerful. She alludes to the insecurities we sometimes feel in shining and being seen, in rising above, and in calling attention to our greatness.

---

[5] This inspiring poem is from Marianne Williamson's book A Return to Love.

In part, Williamson writes:

> *There's nothing enlightened about shrinking*
> *So that other people won't feel insecure around you...*
> *We are all meant to shine...*
> *And as we let our own light shine,*
> *We unconsciously give other people permission to do the same.*
> *As we're liberated from our own fear,*
> *Our presence automatically liberates others.*

I can relate to the feeling of insecurity that arises in shining. I used to feel guilt and shame in laughing with strangers and bantering with people I'd just met because people around me seemed uncomfortable. I worried about what others thought of me and whether my laughter and playfulness would be ill-received. Well, I no longer dim my light.

Chapter 4:

Be Ninja-esque

*O*k, so we've admitted we're uncomfortable meeting strangers, and we're committed to doing it anyway. Where do we start to make it the least painful? Have you ever noticed a greater sense of freedom and openness talking to strangers while out of town or away from your routine than along the course of your usual day where you're likely to see the same people again? Global dating expert Matthew Hussey jokes that you're more likely to talk to a random stranger while laying half-naked poolside at a hotel out of town than fully clothed anywhere close to home. Wonder why that is? There's an immense sense of freedom from our fears when away from our usual environment. It's as though there's an anonymity that accompanies being away from where people might know or recognize you -- not because you want to be scandalous (maybe you do, but this is definitely *not* a book about that). Moreso, this seems due to feeling freer of the consequences of others' judgment!

I'm not proposing that fear of judgment or rejection is simply absent when you're out of town. Your fears are the same whether you're in town or not. But, if you're not going to see the people around you again, the consequence of their judgment or rejection seems less consequential. This is why you'll sometimes witness people acting out of character and saying:

"I'm never going to see them again anyway." It's not necessarily a conscious thought process but if it were, it would likely sound something like, *"Wooo! No one here knows me! No one here will ever see me again. I'm just going to try on different sides of me to see what comes of it! I'm going to let my hair down! Maybe I'll be sassier. Maybe I'll be more playful and laugh out loud more! I can be anyone I want and no one's judgment here matters because I'm simply here today, gone tomorrow!"* That is liberating! This is what I want for you. I want you to be ninja-esque!

A ninja is defined by various sources online as *a person who excels in a skill or activity...is hired for <u>covert</u> purposes...<u>moves and acts without being seen</u>.* Let's be clear. I definitely do not suggest you engage in physical violence, warfare, or espionage. I do propose you have fun with moving and acting without concern for being remembered, at least not for the awkward parts. I want you to feel freer to act in ways that are liberating, fun, and in line with your strengths and gifts. With practice, the skills you develop *will* leave memorable impressions and in wonderful ways over time, but for now, we're going to assume not while you practice wearing new hats. I want you to feel most comfortable in trying out your skills in places where it won't matter if you're clumsy as you practice, where no one there will see you again anyway...and if they do, it'll be because you made a good impression and they chose to!

The safer you feel from the consequence of your fears, the more likely you are to try new ways of creating connections. In the next chapter, you'll begin by practicing direct and engaged eye contact. If you go somewhere new where no one knows you, you'll take the childlike curiosity of wondering what might happen. You have no history there, so you have no baggage to draw from. If you fail to make good eye contact, that's ok. Few, if any, will notice. Few, if any, will remember. But, if you succeed in making and maintaining *warm* eye contact and engage with people as a result, you may very well be remembered in a wonderful way.

Have fun as you go. Imagine each skill as a piece of a costume you're trying on. See how you feel as you try each on in your new settings. Try several times in several new settings. Forget *'never talk to strangers.'* I'd argue, *'always talk to strangers!'* Practice makes progress, so talk to everybody! As the age-old adage goes, 'Don't judge a book by its cover.'[6] The more practice you get in talking to strangers, the more you enhance your comfort in doing so and the more opportunities you'll create for successful, pleasant interactions.

Start emanating your new social aura in an Uber or Lyft ride, bus, or train ride. Talk to the driver or others on the ride. Ask how their day is going, how long they've been on the job, what their favorite part of their work or week is. Heck, ask to hear their favorite story of having picked someone up for a ride! Simply show interest in them. How often have you seen your driver or other riders and immediately assumed you wouldn't enjoy the ride or have anything to talk about? Perhaps you assume you'll have nothing to talk about if someone's outside of a certain age group, or if someone's of a certain gender? Perhaps you've passed judgment on someone based on their dress, jewelry, make-up, or some other observable quality. I'm a strong believer that a person's most redeeming traits can't be seen by the naked eye, so please don't make assumptions based on what you see. Some of the most wonderful, gracious, enjoyable conversations I've had were with people who were most unassuming. Dig deeper.

One of the easiest ways to try on your new ninja-esque skills is by volunteering to greet at an event or serve at the registration table of a charity function. Registration tables allow you to practice cheerful greetings while maintaining patience over multiple moving parts. People attending charity events also tend to be in brighter, more giving spirits and are likely to co-

---

[6] This saying is credited to a 1944 edition of the African Journal American Speech: *"You can't judge a book by its binding."* The saying gained notoriety in its reference in the 1946 murder mystery *Murder in the Glass Room* by Lester Fuller and Edwin Rolfe: "You can never tell a book by its cover."

create a more positive experience as you practice your new skills. The key element is greeting with a smile, enthusiasm, and warmth. Volunteering exposes you to a great number of people you're unlikely to see again, all in one place and with whom you can easily rehearse warm greetings and initial introductions along with other civilities. Thank people for their service and contribution. Ask how they got involved or heard about the event. Notice next time you attend an event that has a registration table how you feel about the people who sit back and passively wait for you to walk up to them and offer your name versus those who enthusiastically call you over, welcome you, thank you for joining, and ask your name. Which would create a more positive experience? Additionally, while volunteering, you'll feel an inherent sense of purpose in your role which invariably makes it easier to greet with confidence and intention. Our actions also tend to feel weightier when done for others than for ourselves so simply giving of your time to serve others is likely to leave you feeling a boost of confidence and joy, which will also affect your confidence in talking to strangers.

One of my favorite poems was written by a remarkable man who runs the Clinic for Visually Impaired Veterans at the hospital where I work. He, himself, is legally blind and one of the most dedicated, compassionate people I've had the pleasure of working with. With his permission, I'd love to share with you his poem, *Seeing Blind.* Tom, you remain an inspiration to me and many others.

To my readers, please consider Tom's words the next time you're getting to know someone. The vision of a leader inspires and draws from within:

Seeing blind I am fearless. The gift of seeing blind for me is what I no longer see.
I see no ugly or poverty. I see no difference or ethnicity.
I do not see fat or skinny. I cannot see short or tall.
I do not see wealth to impress me. I do not see augmented bodies to excite me.
I cannot see broken, sickness, or disability.
I do not see gender, hetero, or homosexuality.
I cannot see your religion to confuse me.
I do not see your country or wars that scare me.
I do not see your bigger house, new car, or flashy jewelry to diminish me.
I do not see weakness or the elderly.
I do not see your education, title, or position to lord over me.
I cannot see injustice that consumes me...
Why do you still feel sorry for me? Seeing blind I see more than you see.

-Tom Hicks

As you rehearse the skills laid out in this text, expect that the first few times with each skill may feel awkward, forced, clumsy, or ineffective...keep trying. Excellence takes extensive practice. You are the only person you control. If you don't change, you will repeat patterns ending up with the same results. You may recognize this as the definition of insanity.[7]

Nonverbal communication is critical to ninjas, especially as they move stealthily through their environments. You want to be intentional with your movements and expressions. As humans, we cannot *not* communicate.

---

[7] Definition of Insanity: Doing the same thing over and over again yet expecting a different result. - *Rita Mae Brown; Einstein*

Everything we do…every action, no matter how small or seemingly insignificant, sends a message that may be interpreted consciously or unconsciously by people around us based on how they experience us. If someone attempts to talk to you and you turn away or turn to talk to someone else, you're communicating unspoken messages. If someone's talking to you and you don't look at them, you're communicating. What are you communicating? Poor listening skills, poor manners, disengagement, and possibly an impression of being judgmental or unkind. The definition of integrity is how you behave when no one's watching. Well, in this case, people may be.

Being a ninja doesn't mean you're invisible. It means putting on your ninja gear…or suit? Cape? Cloak…whatever ninjas wear. *Try it on*, then practice self-focus. Go out of your way to a new part of town you haven't visited and become a student of your own behavior. Allow for awkward beginnings. Create new memories in environments where you have no history. Choose places where you feel you can recreate yourself where no one knows the old you…not because the old you is bad or wrong but simply because you're evolving into an even better, new you.

Practice being more intentional in how you approach others and see how they react to you. You might strategically try on new power colors (see Chapter 16), warm eye contact (see Chapter 5), a toothy smile (see Chapter 6), or a spirit of telling people you meet something you like or appreciate about them as you move about (see Chapters 13 & 14). Making positive changes in these and other ways can noticeably change the way others respond to you and how they feel around you.

Chapter 5:
The Welcome Mat to the Soul

You're probably familiar with the sentiment that the eyes are the windows to the soul? Have you ever noticed how different it feels to talk to someone who's making direct eye contact with you while you speak versus holding conversations while people's eyes wander? Have you noticed how often people either avoid eye contact or repeatedly look away during conversation? Which makes you feel more likely to want to engage and trust? Some cultures see direct eye contact as a sign of disrespect and thus avoiding eye contact may be the norm. I am always a proponent of respecting culture, so I defer to cultural standards in this regard. The following is written, however, for those who see eye contact as a sign of respect, warmth, and trustworthiness. Poor eye contact in these cases can have grave implications for building connections.

Aside from cultural factors, people may avoid eye contact for many reasons. They might be shy or anxious in social settings. They may have difficulties with the emotional intimacy that can feel overwhelming with direct eye contact. They might be too focused on their technology to look up. They may fear direct eye contact as threatening and want to avoid potential discomfort. It's also imperative that we consider they may have a disability, visual or otherwise, that renders eye contact either difficult or impaired. Please be sensitive to this as well. Regardless of one's reasons, the consequence of poor eye contact can be crippling on connecting with strangers and creating positive first impressions. If I had to choose one skill that has been most impactful in my ability to connect with strangers, it's regulation of the area around my eyes to exude cheer and warmth. Incidentally, I even teach blind patients to look in the direction of a voice even if they can't see the speaker. The mere impression of eye contact in these patients has resulted in increased connectedness to others, more intimate bonding, and overall improvements in mood.

Consider for a moment crow's feet, which are the lines that form around the outer sides of your eyes and radiate out. The younger you are, the less pronounced these may be, but you'll likely still notice lines when you laugh. The deeper and more frequently you laugh, the more pronounced these lines are likely to be. Some use Botox and anti-aging products to reduce these lines. I may use eye cream, but I still love these lines as a crowning glory of joy. Have you noticed when you 'fake-smile,' the area around your eyes doesn't move nearly as much as if you're sincerely smiling, laughing, or giggling? Seldom do people think of this area when talking about the impact of smiling, and yet these lines and movements represent genuine heartfelt joy. Try it for yourself. When I let out a hearty laugh, it's almost like my eyes entirely shut and the area around my eyes looks clenched. When I fake smile, the area around my lips and mouth move, but there's little movement around my eyes. Additionally, when I fake smile you seldom see my teeth. There is a noticeable difference in how you'll feel when fake-smiling versus sincerely smiling *with your eyes*. The movement of the area around the eyes, therefore, is a beautiful gift. I hope you'll embrace it!

Direct eye contact when first meeting people is especially powerful. It can feel inviting and conveys confidence, and confidence is attractive! Many notice a harder time trusting people who avoid eye contact, find it more difficult to connect with them, and feel a lesser sense of emotional intimacy when eye contact is poor. Eye contact tends to activate curiosity in others, and curiosity drives engagement and intrigue.

Please use caution in overcompensating with eye contact. If too intense or prolonged, eye contact can be off-putting. It may seem menacing, odd, or condescending. Have you ever noticed how awkward 3 seconds or more of eye contact can feel? Try it! It's awkward! Find the sweet spot around eye contact that lets people know you're open and warm without being off-putting. Couple eye contact with a smile and you're far more likely to engage others.

Another way to regulate eye contact to let others know you're interested in speaking with them is to catch someone's gaze, hold it for just a second or two, smile, look away, then look back. Matthew Hussey, an entertaining and skilled dating coach for women, agrees this is a playful, coy way of showing interest in someone, certainly in the dating arena. I invite you to search online for his videos on eye contact. Eye contact can be a not-so subtle way of engaging others while successfully facilitating dialogue even if you're too shy to walk over and initiate yourself. The double glance-over is a great way of letting someone know you'd be interested in interacting. Use caution: you may also be sending a message of romantic interest with this technique so use it wisely.

Interestingly, within an hour of writing this chapter, I was walking down the clothing aisle toward the check-out counters in a department store. Repeatedly other shoppers avoided eye contact altogether or made eye contact then quickly looked down and away...unless I smiled and caught their gaze.

Each time I did this, they smiled back, and their posture changed. They stood up straighter and taller. Tell me that's not a powerful impact.

In short, don't underestimate the power of eye contact, especially coupled with a friendly smile and greeting. It's simply laying out the welcome mat that starts the road to the soul. Certainly, there's much more to building a lasting relationship, but it's a step in the right direction. Simply put, eye contact lets others know you're friendly and confident in your approachability and likely to welcome interactions.

Chapter 6:

Bring the Light

I nearly combined this chapter on smiling with the one on eye contact because the two go critically hand-in-hand to emanate sincere expressions of warmth. One without the other may send incongruent messages, yet each is independently vital.

It's imperative to distinguish between different types of smiles because not every smile is received equally. Some smiles are warm and engaging; others come across as menacing and off-putting. Be the person that people feel more comfortable and safe approaching. Be the person others notice, not because of superficial looks but because you disarm them with warmth and personality. Be the person who gets others to smile or laugh, not by being a clown but by infusing playfulness and lightheartedness everywhere you go.

It may seem odd to consider any type of smile as less than warm, but if content and context are incongruent, a smile can quickly feel threatening, manipulative, or intimidating. Content is *what* is said, whereas context is the *how, where, and when* it is presented. If both are congruent, the smile seems sincere. So, if I smile while letting you know I enjoyed our conversation, that is consistent and feels sincere. If, however, I smile or smirk in response to a comment or situation that would normally evoke a neutral or negative reaction, I may come across as sarcastic, rude, condescending, or insulting. You'll usually find this sort of response in people with insecurities. They may chuckle while giving you feedback about something they don't like or smile when upset rather than express themselves directly with words. This type of response can feel distancing, passive-aggressive, and piercingly painful to the recipient. I'd recommend you steer clear of the sinister smirk and incongruent deliveries. It's hard to predict the effect a certain type of smile will have on communication until it's experienced, but I think it's safe to say smile when something feels good and don't when it doesn't.

A laugh, giggle, or smile showing teeth can quickly disarm people, especially in response to playful or endearing comments. Some sideways grins can seem coy or flirtatious. Full smiles with eyes averted down and to the side can likewise communicate flirtation or interest, especially in response to ambiguous or suggestable comments, so beware.

The most engaging type of smile involves lips widely outstretched, teeth showing, face muscles in movement—a genuine, disinhibited expression of joy. My beautiful mother in this photo is portraying one of the most beautiful smiles I've seen. Notice everything in her face moves up as she shows joy.

Some people don't smile due to insecurities about their teeth. In these cases, or if you suspect this might be the case, please show compassion and grace, and withhold judgment or assumptions about hygiene. We don't know others' stories. It always hurts my heart when I hear people comment on others' teeth because they don't know that person's history and what they've overcome in their lives. Let's be among the people of the world who focus on strengths and building others up, not on imperfections, judgment, or breaking others down. You might think, "Well, I'd never say it out loud." Thinking negative thoughts is still discharging your judgments into the Universe, and it's unkind. Please join me in celebrating blessings and helping to shine others' lights.

How soon you simile at someone in an initial encounter is as important as timing in making eye contact, especially in first impressions. Both can predict how comfortable others will feel around you. Most people, whether they admit or realize it, want to be liked. This is often true regardless of their opinion of the other person. When you smile, the person you smile at is more likely to feel liked by you. They're also more likely to like *you* when you're smiling. If you don't smile, it's not unusual for others to wonder what you're thinking and/or assume you don't like them or that you're unapproachable. Much of this can be avoided by simply smiling in the initial greeting or when meeting someone's eyes across a room.

Do you know yourself well enough to know if you have RBF (see Chapter 2 if you missed how I discovered my RBF)? Not sure? Are you often told to smile or asked why you're not smiling? Do people tell you your facial expressions are 'serious' or that you're 'hard to read?' Or, do others often assume you don't like them or ask whether you do? These are usual tells that you may have RBF. But, don't fret. There are countless ways you can consciously regulate your mood (or at least your face) in advance of an event to increase the likelihood of being received more positively.

I want to be clear. I'm not saying it's your responsibility to manage how others feel. It is your responsibility, though, to manage yourself. If you want more pleasant, positive interactions, it would behoove you to address RBF. If you knew that subtly shifting your facial expression, smiling, or making better eye contact could help others feel more at ease around you, bring out the best in you both, or attract others to you, would you make these changes?

Adjusting facial expressions involves minor tweaks in your expressions in advance of an interaction. It may feel fake at first, but it'll feel more natural as you naturally feel the benefits. It's forcing a smile while meeting someone's glance, it's changing your facial expression as you talk/listen to someone, it's moving your eyebrows in response to conversation, it's nodding your head to let someone know you're listening. Ever heard the saying, "Fake it 'til you make it?" This applies here.

The *expression* of your mood when entering an event is vital in whether you give off a positive, welcoming energy or negative, distancing one. Notice, I said *expression of,* not your actual mood. Whether you make eye contact or smile is intimately tied to the expression of your mood. Consciously adjust your mindset to one of positivity and curiosity beforehand. Your face will follow. You're simply training new behaviors until patterns that may feel fake initially become your new *real* expressions.

If you're really not in the mood to smile or present positively, you can give yourself an intentional mood boost on the way to going out by listening to inspirational seminars or music, listening to standup comedy for laughs, watching a YouTube video on "meeting strangers in a crowded room," calling a friend you enjoy joking around with, listening to upbeat music, doing a Zumba routine or yoga before leaving your home, etc.

There are several factors that, when ignored, can dampen positivity. Addressing these immediately will also help. You can recall these by the acronym *H.A.L.T.* often used in mental health and recovery communities to promote improved self-awareness and impulse control. H.A.L.T. stands for *Hungry, Angry, Lonely, Tired.* If you feel any of these, you're less likely to present warmly and openly, so address these needs as best as you can before going out to meet new people. Have a snack, call an inspiring friend, journal or do something healthy to soothe your mood, get a massage, take a nap, etc. A favorite of mine is to program your cell phone to send you a daily alert that reads an inspirational or loving message to uplift your spirits, like "Hello beautiful," "You are loved," or perhaps a message to deliver while you're at an event saying, "Keep talking, keep smiling, you're doing great." You might also subscribe to any one of the many e-mail subscriptions for positive messages from the Universe.

If a spontaneous smile still feels too uncomfortable, find someone to compliment. Perhaps someone has great heels on, a fun tie, a lovely dress, a great hairstyle or a certain color that is flattering. Tell them so. Seeing the positive effect of a compliment on another person is a quick-and-easy way to evoke a smile in you both. Incidentally, it is a far greater compliment to tell someone "You make that color look great" or "You look great in that color" vs "That color looks great on you." Just be sincere.

Want to know a trick for an easy way to get someone to smile or laugh? Tell them you love their smile or laugh! Caution #1: *This could be awkward if they haven't smiled or laughed yet...* Caution #2: *One of the worst things you can say to someone who's not smiling is a comment pointing this out, like "why aren't you smiling?" or telling them "smile."* This only points out their discomfort, typically leaves them feeling more self-conscious, uncomfortable, and far less likely to want to engage with you.

If you feel unnatural smiling at first, use your eyes and the rest of your face to engage. My own history with RBF changed as I started to consciously change my facial expression from one of disengagement when nervous or confused to one of childlike awe. What do I mean by this? When I feel confused or unsure of something nowadays, I find myself with my mouth open yet still forming a smile, my eyebrows pulled up in curiosity, and a playful expression of openness to surprise! I would imagine I look like someone who just walked in on her own surprise party, ready to laugh out but not yet sure what's going on. This sounds more awkward than it appears. I'm certain it gives off a laughable, welcoming, pleasant look moreso than the more serious, closed-off expressions of my past. In these moments, my whole energy shifts to one of feeling joy and readiness for excitement. Having trained myself to show up this way in novel situations contributes to an air of positive energy. It has also invited much humor, banter, and fun into my world.

Incidentally, you know yawns are contagious, right? Well, I'd argue smiling has a similar contagious effect. As hard as it is to resist yawning when you see another person yawn, it can be equally as difficult to resist smiling when someone in proximity smiles. I wonder, if smiles are contagious and yawns are contagious, are mouth movements in general contagious? Are you contorting your face now to see if you can come up with entertaining facial movements to try in a social experiment? No? Just me? Ok, moving on.

One more point of caution about facial expressions before we move on: Under times of duress whether sadness, anger, stress, irritation or other negative feeling, it's not unusual to revert back to your "used-to-be" facial expression. Please be extra careful to notice what your face is doing or 'saying' when you're having a difficult day or moment. Be sure your world isn't mirroring back to you what you're giving off.

If you ever question your impact on the world, smile. Smile at one person then another until one smiles back. There's your impact. You might just be the only one that person felt noticed by or smiled with that day. Some of my favorite moments are in getting other drivers to smile back at me in traffic. Better than that is when I engage them to start laughing across lanes with a complete stranger and without words! What a great way to lighten stress in the world. Random connections like this are exhilarating!

One of my favorite quotes is by Bill Wilson, "*To the world, you may be one person, but to one person you may be the world.*[8]" Generously share your smile. Consider your power. Show others you're a safe zone, unlikely to reject

---

[8] Incidentally, this quote is attributed to several other authors, including Dr. Seuss.

them and ready to receive them warmly; be that. A genuinely warm smile can metaphorically light up a room, so bring the light my friends! Enter a room with your head held high, make eye contact with whoever you pass and smile. Make sure your cheekbones move up…even better if your teeth show. Then, watch how others respond. People remember those who bring out their smile, *especially* when they don't want to.

Chapter 7:
Tone of Voice and Posture

*I*f you're old enough to remember Ben Stein, the Economic Teacher who droned on as he took attendance in the movie *Ferris Bueller's Day Off*, enough said. If not, he's a YouTube search away: "Bueller… Bueller…"

We've all met people whose speaking style is monotone, seldom inflecting their tone up or down. It can be emotionally taxing to be in dialogue with someone whose tone doesn't change. Inflection can be easily learned and unquestionably impactful. Tone of voice and posture are both highly suggestive of confidence and comfort. Both can either enhance the strength of an interaction or detract from an impression, so regulating them differently can affect interactions.

Any behavioral change can be learned, and *people will change if they want to and if their commitment to change is strong enough*. If you want to change a pattern, you can and will. If you don't want to, you'll come up with every excuse for why you *can't, won't, or shouldn't*. Did you know that even sleep is considered a trainable behavior? Pattern of speech is a behavior, smiling and eye contact are behaviors, standing up straight is a behavior, eating is a behavior, exercise is a behavior, dating style is a behavior, kissing style is a behavior…you get the drift.

Tone of voice and posture are especially noticeable in initial greetings. If you went to see a doctor who was meek in tone, would it impact how you feel? Meek tones can be interpreted as passive or insecure. Would you feel confident in the care of a provider whose voice trembles or who speaks so softly you can barely hear what is said? How about if the doctor slouches each time you visit? Would that help or hurt your sense of comfort in the care you'll receive? Now, imagine you're at an event assessing whether you want to do business with others there. Would you be more or less likely to engage with someone if you had to ask them to repeat themselves several times because you couldn't hear what they said? On the other hand, loud and boisterous styles can also be negatively interpreted as arrogant, showy, or intimidating.

The sweet spot seems to fall in sounding pleasant and chipper in an initial greeting, inflecting up rather than down and quickly softening in tone to one of a more controlled yet still confident cadence as the conversation continues. What do I mean by inflecting up? Inflecting up *as you complete a sentence* involves varying the pitch of what is said to sound slightly higher pitched as you say the *last word or phrase*, giving an impression of interest. Emphasis on inflection is on the last syllable stated. Imagine how different your experience of meeting strangers would be if you introduced yourself to everyone as though you're reuniting with your best friend from years ago: "Hi [insert name]! I'm thrilled/delighted to meet you!"

Inflecting down, by the way, can be used strategically as well. In initial greetings, it can sound subdued or monotone, even Eeyore-like,[9] which might distance others leaving them less interested to engage. However, inflecting down can also be used to express compassion or regret in response to sad or disappointing news or to effectively end a conversation.

---

[9] *Eeyore* is a character and friend of Winnie-the-Pooh from the book series by A. A. Milne. Eeyore is an old grey stuffed donkey, often depicted as pessimistic, gloomy, and depressed.

Before moving on from voice, please consider a caution involving speaking too loud. If others repeatedly glance your way without smiling or talking to you, it may be an indication that you're too loud or the tone of your voice is off-putting. They might also be attracted to you and nervous, but less likely if more than one person looks your way in the same way. Either way, do a quick self-assessment.

Posture is especially powerful in engaging conversation. I *lean in* as I listen to people speak, especially if they're speaking of something sensitive, intimate, or difficult. Leaning in gives the subtle message that I'm fully engaged and attending carefully to what's being said, that I care. As before, maintaining direct eye contact is vital. Leaning away or turning my feet away from the person I'm in dialogue with gives the impression I'm disengaged or only partially engaged and preparing my getaway.

Other ways whereby I invite more conversation include smiling and nodding. Doing so welcomes a person to continue speaking. I inflect without a wide range, meaning I vary my tone without getting too loud or too soft. I smile, giggle, and laugh unless to do so would be incongruent with what we're speaking of. It is obvious from my nonverbals that can be seen from anywhere in a room that I'm at least friendly, pleasant, and willing to engage. Up close, I want whoever I'm talking to at any given moment to feel they're the only person who matters in that moment, and my voice communicates that I am pleased to meet them, confident in the conversation, and listening.

Before we move on, let's talk about things you might say to leave others with positive feelings in chance encounters. I value being a student of my behaviors and in writing this book have been especially attentive to how I speak to salesclerks. A clerk recently asked if I'd like a bag for what I'd purchased. I didn't just say "yes" or "yah" (which, by the way, is a pet peeve; 'yah' just sounds lazy). I made direct eye contact with her, smiled, and replied, "Yes please, if you don't mind. Thank you so much for asking!"

This may sound cumbersome, but it's well worth a few extra seconds to show sincere gratitude, to honor someone's assistance, and to let supervisors know of their staff's efforts. I'm sure this is received differently than a simple one-word reply. I notice how often clerks seem undervalued by rushed or distracted shoppers, and I commit to treating each one with respect and appreciation. I'm even known to call store managers after my experience to let them know of staff who went above and beyond in their service.

Next time you're leaving a store, instead of simply saying "Bye" or "Thanks," try saying, "I so appreciate you, thank you for your help" or "Thank you so much. I hope you have a lovely night." This is an instance when I'd say less is *not* more.

Chapter 8:
Remember Thy Name

*T*here are a few things I'll never forget about initial impressions that I learned at a seminar years ago. 1) Dale Carnegie said that a "person's name is to that person the sweetest and most important sound in any language" universally, and 2) a great strategy for remembering someone's name is to repeat it three times at first introduction. For example, "Hi Jeremy! It's so nice to meet you, Jeremy. Where did you grow up Jeremy?" That might sound forced or artificial but in context works quite well.

Imagine how it feels when someone you just met remembered your name a moment later. Now, imagine how it feels when someone you met weeks, months, or even years ago runs into you and remembers your name. I don't know about you, but I feel pleasantly surprised and somewhat in-awe. It is quite impressive when someone has both the skill and interest in you to retain something so personal as your name. There are many seminars and books on strategies for improving your skills at remembering names, and I highly recommend looking into them.

It's not uncommon for people to blame forgetting someone's name on a poor memory. How often have you met someone who forgot your name then said: "I'm just awful with names," thinking this released them of offense. It doesn't. Everyone wants to feel memorable, and it's *not* an excuse to blame a poor memory. I'm still no expert at remembering names but I'm sincerely apologetic if I miss it. I'll own up to it, ask again, and refuse to diminish the importance or excuse my faux pas by blaming memory.

There are countless mnemonic strategies on affiliating names with different associations to help retain increasingly more names in a small period of time. They did recommend against affiliating names with actors given a higher likelihood of confusing the person's name with different roles the actor has played and/or the wrong parts of the actors' names.

Another suggestion regarding names is to be sure to ask a person what name they prefer to go by, then respect and honor that. And for heaven's sake, please don't change someone's name because you can't pronounce it. Make the effort, let them know it's important to you that you address them as they would like to be addressed, and show them respect by learning. I can't tell you how many people I know with multisyllabic, ethnically-diverse names who go by abbreviated names like Sherry or Tom for the ease of the English-speaker. I'm certain these are not even close to their real names. It makes me sad to think people may be diminishing their identity to fit into mainstream culture when we all deserve to be honored precisely as we are.

Chapter 9:
Show Curiosity

I'm amazed at how often I meet people who seem to have little to no awareness of how they communicate with others. They'll talk and talk until they're done talking, then they wait to be asked the next question so they can talk more. It doesn't seem to occur to them to volley back a question and engage others in talking as well. The impression they leave others with is that they have an agenda or quota to meet and others are simply there to serve them. Some, if challenged, will say they don't want to be intrusive so don't ask questions and instead wait for others to volunteer information. I don't recommend this. Part of what connects us is the feeling that someone has taken an interest in us. Prepare at least a few thoughtful questions to participate in fluid conversation.

I'm also amazed at how often others are unaware of their pattern of complaining about events. They tend not to realize how off-putting their verbal and nonverbal behaviors can be. Instead of showing curiosity into their own patterns and why they are not approached, they make assumptions and criticize others as weak and poor at communicating/engaging. I like to think I do this differently. I frequently ask myself how my presentation may be helping or hurting my connection with others.

One of the most important points to stress in this section is that you *listen and actively engage.* Some people are passive recipients of life. They wait for opportunities to come *to* them. I challenge you to create life and memories everywhere you go! At a minimum, please, for the love of whoever your Higher Power is, if someone initiates a conversation with you, put your cell phone aside, make eye contact with them, and smile. Act as if they matter to you for at least a moment in time.

Sometimes people ignore opportunities for passing conversations because they're busy or distracted. Sometimes they assume the conversation will go nowhere. When you assume a conversation won't be fruitful, you are likely making a snap judgment based on superficial assessment. Please resist the urge to judge another person's appearance, dress, status, work, pastime, etc. Doing so is simply unkind and rude. Everyone has value, and if you decide someone's not worth your time because they don't immediately look like someone you'd like to engage with, you're going to attract that same judgmental, negative energy into your life, and frankly, you're not being nice. I am sad to have to stress this point, yet I see it all the time. Some of my favorite interactions have been with people who may have initially been overlooked had I been comparing them to a hypothetical mold in my mind of who I wanted to meet. Consider the possibility that the Universe makes NO mistakes. How different would life be if you treated every chance encounter as one that is here to teach you or another person a life lesson? *Sometimes it's not just about us.* Maybe you're an instrument in the Universe's grand plan.

As far as feeling busy, I'd like to strongly encourage you to refrain from saying so. Have you noticed how it feels when you ask people how they're doing and they reply, "Busy! I'm just so busy" with little else to say? Telling people how busy you are instills negativity and distance in conversations and can curtail dialogue. We're all busy, yet we can make time for moments in time. I bet you'd find time if the opportunity for a hot date popped up while you were *so busy*! Telling people how busy you are does not raise your social value or significance. In many cases, it makes you seem unapproachable, arrogant, and challenged around time management, so try a different response. Instead, share about what's kept you busy: "I've been working on writing a book, learning to ski, learning another language, traveling, volunteering at the dog shelter" or any other truth. This facilitates direction for further questions and conversation about mutually shared interests. By the way, ask follow-up questions to whatever the person just told you about. Not only will this show you were listening and curious but also engages more dialogue about something the other person enjoys, which tends to bring out the best in people.

Showing curiosity is about asking questions more than making statements. It's about entering a room enthusiastically as though everyone there can teach you something. Sometimes the lesson is how *not* to behave. The easiest way to spark a conversation with a stranger is to ask about a preference: "Would you recommend the marble loaf or banana nut bread?" Or, "What do you think, iced coffee or hot latte?" Another option is to include a sincere compliment, "I love your perfume/cologne. May I ask what scent or brand it is?" These icebreakers let others know you're friendly, fun, and engageable. Hussey incidentally recommends that asking a favor can inspire others to reciprocate connecting behaviors such as, "Would you mind watching my jacket for a moment?" This sets the stage comfortably for a conversation upon your return, as you extend thanks for the favor. This all helps set the platform for welcoming others to engage more comfortably.

Other great questions to ask, especially at business networking events, include those that evoke emotion or passion. Examples are "What's your secret for being good at what you do?" Or, "What's something you're passionate about?" Another would be, "What brings out the happy little kid in you?" Or, "If time, judgment, and finances didn't matter, how would you live life differently?"

Motivational speaker and relationship coach Kute Blackson proposes that women ask potential courters, "What is your purpose in life?" before agreeing to share their phone number or go on a date! Intimidating, but meaningful! These questions may sound pointed but can reveal a person's core values and intent, which is a great tell as to your compatibility if you wish for any kind of relationship beyond a casual, passing encounter.

By the way, questions don't have to be about the other person. Questions could simply be general conversation-starters that help open dialogue, such as "I'm sorry to trouble you, is this table by you open?" or "Excuse me, do you happen to know where the restrooms are?" As I was writing this chapter, someone had left a nearly full, yet watered-down coffee drink on the windowsill by an open table in Starbucks. I asked the gentleman sitting at the neighboring table if he knew if the person was coming back. We agreed it was safe to sit, then exchanged jokes about what a waste it was to leave a full drink. We agreed we'd have split it if that didn't sound germ-ridden. We shared a laugh and returned to our work. Memorable moment achieved.

One of my favorite ways to inspire questions when I feel at a loss or when going on a long drive with a friend or loved one is to google 'questions to get to know [fill in the blank with relationship, e.g., mother, best friend, boyfriend, new person, etc.].' It's a fun way to build curiosity and adventure into your relationships and can just as easily be incorporated in new connections. You, of course, wouldn't pull out your phone to access lists of questions while introducing yourself to strangers. You might, however, have a few questions saved to your phone or memorized, to ask people you've just met, or you might pull up a list of questions to have fun with if several folks have just met and are waiting together for an event to start. This would depend on the crowd but can be a fun way to insert playfulness and lightheartedness.

Questions open and engage dialogue and incite interest in deepening a relationship. Statements tend to shorten or end dialogue. If you attempt to ask several questions and the conversation seems forced, one-sided, or awkward, no problem. Simply move on to the next person with whom you might have a more natural rhythm. If the first person really wishes to connect with you, they now know you're friendly and kind and they can return to find you and (hopefully) participate more in a conversation. You decide, though, if this is someone you're naturally in alignment with as a friend, colleague, or otherwise.

We often attempt to force relationships that don't naturally feel good and *let others pick us instead of doing the picking* because it seems the path of least resistance. Be mindful of whether you're fostering genuine connections with people. Forced connections are much harder to grow and maintain in a meaningful way. I'd recommend if it's not flowing, redirect your energy toward people who are in alignment with you and who you want to attract so the connections feel authentic.

One of the easiest places to spark conversations with strangers is at the airport! You got it, "Where are you traveling to? What takes you there?" You might ask if they've been there before or what their favorite travel destination has been. Practice asking questions of every person you sit by but keep moving about. People are often their most open and engaging when on their way out of town for vacation, so airports are great fertile ground for practice!

Here are a few questions to get you thinking about whether you're a good listener and engaging when talking to strangers. Do you look away when someone's talking to you? What does your body language communicate? Is your body turned toward or away from the person you're in conversation with? Are you checking the time while talking to someone? These are cues that can be seen across a room that may give others information on your manners and whether you're an active, engaged listener. You might be someone who 'listens better' when looking away from the person who's talking, but it's not going to look that way to others. Managing social impressions is critical in first impressions. Remember that other people in the room may be watching and evaluating you on how you treat others before deciding how best and whether to engage you. Just a reminder, I'm not suggesting you manage your behaviors to manipulate a desired outcome but rather that you create habits of treating everyone with respect, openness, and warmth in a nondiscriminatory manner that can be seen across a room.

If you do notice you are talking more than listening, you may be spending too much time speaking about what *you* have to offer and how much *you* know to demonstrate competence, value, likeability, or credibility rather than engaging others to share. Others will be more drawn to you if you treat *them* as important and show interest in *them*. We often trust people who *show* us who they are rather than *tell* us who they are. Incidentally, questions also help identify the core of who and how someone is. The *core* of a person is not necessarily who they represent in a first meeting but rather who you understand them to be as time, patterns, and a relationship build.

Author Michael P. Nichols (2009) of *The Lost Art of Listening* provides humbling examples of critical and active listening skills and distractions to listening. He suggests that when you find yourself thinking of the next thing you want to say while someone's talking, you're not listening. *When you tell a related story of your own as soon as the other person is finished talking, you send the message that you're not really listening. You actually hijacked their story and made it about you under the guise that you are relating.* This one's a huge pet peeve of mine and one of the most common social faux pas I see. The listener is almost always well-intentioned, simply wanting to show understanding, but ends up leaving the other person feeling undervalued and invalidated.

Directing conversation to focus on another person takes skill and care. Again, talk less and listen more. *Listen mindfully and patiently and with interest. Drop your agenda.* Maintain eye contact while listening, as it communicates interest. Let the other finish before you start speaking. Do not interrupt even (and especially) if you disagree with what's being said. I often respond when in disagreement with a statement like, "I can appreciate your perspective. I feel differently." If you are interested in learning more about the person's thoughts you may add, "I'd be curious to learn more about your understanding or experience." You also might respond, "Yes, and..." then elaborate with your perspective. Avoid the use of "but" at all costs. The word "but" negates any message before it. Listen to what is being said before preparing a response. Nichols captures the essence of listening beautifully when he says, "Listening is not a need we have; it is a gift we give."

A few final notes on the wisdom of a curious spirit were inspired in a church sermon the week I started writing this book; divine timing is magnificent. The wise person was described as one who arrests judgment and welcomes learning from others. Pastor Preston of Gateway Church described 1) wise people as quiet. The person who talks the most is almost never the person who knows the most. Wise people know the value of silence and the value of words. He joked even fools appear intelligent with their mouths shut. Please don't mistake this as having no opinion. It's about listening more than you talk and being thoughtful with what you say. He described the best time to speak as after having paused to listen for inner wisdom on what to share. He suggested wise people don't have fewer words but are better at how and when to use them. 2) Wise people were described as humble. With humility comes wisdom and willingness to accept help. 3) Wise people were said to be teachable, willing to admit they don't know.

The most teachable spirits are most liked by wise people and said to show prize and value in what wisdom they're given. 4) The wise were said to walk with the wise and at the wise person's pace, not at their own. Pastor added that people often want what they want in their time. He presented humility as wanting wisdom from another, walking in submission of the other. He added that if you want the wisdom of the wise, be willing to accept that wisdom on the wise person's terms with graciousness and gratitude. If a mentor can only offer 1-2 hours of mentorship a year, accept that with appreciation rather than resentment or demand for more time or frequency. The latter is deemed entitlement. Finally, 5) the wise person craves constructive criticism that empowers and builds one up. *Be that type of person.*

Chapter 10:
Lead with Emotional Intelligence

*D*iscomfort, anxiety, pain, joy, jealousy, curiosity, sadness, excitement, hope, enthusiasm, anger, and amazement are all among
healthy, normal ranges of emotions we experience in the human
condition at some time or another. Each emotion provides us with
information on how we are doing in life and whether we would benefit
from changing or maintaining whatever brought on the emotions. Feelings
are not bad, nor should we do away with them. As we work *through* each
emotion, we are afforded a gift; a gift of strength, humility, honesty, and
courage. One of my favorite poems, *The Guest House* by Rumi, speaks to
inviting all emotions in as guides. Rumi suggests welcoming feelings and
treating each honorably as a guest arriving to share wisdom or gifts. I extend
this to imagining an enlightening chat with each emotion over an imaginary
cup of tea or a snack and learning what each has come to teach you.

It's important to monitor how and when we express our feelings.
Emotional intelligence comes in especially handy here. A quick internet
search defines emotional intelligence as the capacity to be aware of, control,
and express one's emotions safely, and to handle interpersonal relationships
judiciously and empathically. Empathy is commonly defined as the ability
to understand and share another's feelings. Emotional intelligence then

involves not only managing how you express yourself around others but also how you respond to and understand others' feelings. Emotional intelligence is central to understanding the difference between intention and impact. Why do I bring this up?

How often have you been talking to someone who tells you about a difficult life circumstance? Maybe a hard day or week? A roadblock at work? A physical ailment, perhaps? Now, how often have you replied starting with the words "At least…"? Brene Brown does a beautiful job of modeling empathic statements in her YouTube video titled Empathy. She explains that empathic statements rarely start with the words, "At least…" It's not empathic to say, "At least the day's almost over." It's not empathic to say, "At least you have a job." It's not empathic to say, "At least you look good" or, "At least you were still able to make it out." The intention of the words, "At least…" seem usually more about transitioning away from uncomfortable dialogue. The impact of this seems often minimizing of another's feelings. Responding with "At least," then, says more about your discomfort in being there for another person and your difficulty thinking of helpful words to validate than about the other person's experience. Brown (2012) suggests in channeling empathy that you connect, before responding, to a part of you that has experienced similar feelings to what someone shares. She also offers the option of saying, "I don't know what to say, but I am really glad you told me" instead of an "At least" response.

You might be thinking people shouldn't be commenting on their bad day when meeting someone for the first time. To that, I'd first say, "Stop should'ing" over yourself. People are people, and it's natural to want to connect and feel heard on bad days as much if not more than on good days. It may even be more memorable to feel engaged by others on days when you don't feel good or don't feel like smiling than when you're already having a great day and smiling. Is telling strangers your woes a great idea? No, it can give the impression of unhealthy boundaries, but it does happen, and if you're the recipient of this, I encourage you to practice grace and compassion before moving on. Show respect to others for however they present. You don't have to like what you see or want a relationship if you don't feel in alignment but allowing space for others to show up and feel accepted authentically is simply kind. You can politely excuse yourself to a bathroom and on to the next conversation once you've extended civility.

Emotional intelligence is enhanced as you work toward excellence in perspective-taking, putting yourself in others' shoes. Extending compassion is a high-value virtue and connects us. You never know what hurts people are carrying. Perhaps you're encountering certain people to serve value in their lives or help get their minds off something painful for a moment in time. Consider again, it's not always about you, and often it isn't. Thank whoever you meet simply for sharing with you.

If you are frequently met with discomfort across social situations, I challenge you to consider that what you attract is often a mirror of what you give off. What might that be? You may think you're engaging, tactful, and socially adept. It's easy to blame failed connections on the awkwardness of situations, intimidating nature of events, or general unease in new situations where you're competing with others for attention. That attitude, however, won't help you create a different experience or attract more positive connections. It's ok to acknowledge discomfort in crowded events or traditional networking. Choose also to be the light you want to attract.

Develop a plan for where you'll practice your new skills that's different from what you're already doing in a way that embraces growth rather than overwhelms you. Create a list of 10 uncomfortable social scenarios ranked least to most uncomfortable, a fear hierarchy if you will. Slowly start working your way up the list, practicing your new skills in each environment. Develop a new, more exciting relationship with each new experience. So much of this practice and growth come from state of mind and what you tell yourself.

Let's go over a few specific 'no-no's' of communication. These are especially helpful to consider in interacting with strangers but also good practice across-the-board. I would discourage you from starting questions with the word "why." Why, do you ask? Starting questions with the word 'why' can evoke defensiveness. Doing so tends to be received as a questioning of the other person or an attack, even when innocuous. Likewise, the word 'but' can be a communication barrier. The word 'but' tends to negate anything that came before it, no matter how positive. For example, if you said, "It was great meeting you, but..." You may have no intention of saying anything negative about the meeting. Nevertheless, the initial pleasantry is diminished, even if the statement were to end, "It was great meeting you, but the steak was a bit overdone." Not only are you now confused, but you're also left with a less positive impression of the connection. Use of the word 'but' sounds like rejection about to happen.

Avoid extremes, like 'always' and 'never.' These also tend to evoke defensiveness, may trigger conflict, and can come across as extreme, emotional, or dramatic. Before you know it, you're arguing about one exception to the extreme, and the underlying concern is diluted or lost altogether. I also caution you to *be careful, not crushing* in how you talk about others, especially in new connections or in times of disagreement. Avoid negative or deprecating comments about people or events, or you'll run the risk of being seen as negative, judgmental, or gossipy. Instead, assume the best in others, and keep it positive or at a minimum neutral. Emotional intimacy and trust take time to build, and it's unwise to share openly views that may be critical or controversial in initial meetings.

True connection cannot exist without emotional intimacy, vulnerability, and realness. It is invaluable to extend grace in meeting new people who are different from us. It is likewise important to be slow to judge. Carnegie (981) wrote that we're typically not dealing with creatures of logic but rather creatures of emotion, bristling with prejudices, judgments, and motivated by pride and vanity. *If you choose your battles wisely, you'll be far more effective in winning those that matter and accepting those that don't.* Welcome whoever you meet to show up as their authentic selves. Acceptance does not mean you like what you see or wish to commit to a lifelong relationship. It means respect for differences.

In *The Velveteen Rabbit*, Margery Bianco (1922) brought to life nicely the point of accepting others for their authentic selves. She wrote of a conversation between the Velveteen Rabbit and the old Skin Horse who lived together among the nursery toys. The Horse with his brown coat, bald in patches and seams showing underneath, had lived longer than any of the other stuffed animals. He told the Rabbit tales of toys becoming real through the love of children. When the Rabbit asked what made someone real, the Horse responded that '*real*' isn't how one is made but rather a thing that happens over time and life, not to be feared or avoided. He spoke to pain and loss that accompany life and freedom and intimacy that come with feeling accepted exactly as you are. I quote, in part:

"By the time you are Real, most of your hair has been loved off…
your eyes drop out and you get loose in the joints…
But these things don't matter… because
Once you are Real you can't be ugly,
except to people who don't understand."
- The Velveteen Rabbit

Chapter 11:

Dress for Success

*T*his is one of those chapters you'd think would be common sense, but I've come to find it simply isn't. I find people typically lie at either end of two camps. One group tends to argue they shouldn't be judged by their attire and that their credibility, capabilities, skill sets, and work ethic should speak for themselves. You'll seldom find this person dressed in formal attire or close-toed shoes other than sneakers, let alone slacks or a suit and tie. It's not unusual for this person to arrive to work or social functions in tennis shoes and/or flip flips. I'll admit, having grown up in Washington, D.C., a mecca for political types who were often dressed to the nines, I'm biased here. By the way, anyone know where the saying 'dressed to the nines' came from? I didn't, so I googled it. Wikipedia says: *"To the nines" is an English idiom meaning "to perfection" or "to the highest degree."* That's about right.

I in no way assert that the only way to make a positive impression is by over-dressing everywhere you go or by own a suit or formal gown. I do propose that it can send a very different message in *first* impressions when you choose the long-sleeved, button-down shirt or blouse over the t-shirt; when you choose the fitted shirt over the one that is several sizes too large; a tie or accessory over none; slacks over shorts or jeans; or dress shoes over tennis shoes or sandals. Of course, neighborhood, setting, and safety considerations might influence your presentation. You wouldn't want to wear dangly items that could be strangulation risks or dress up to walk around alone in dark or potentially unsafe areas, but I might argue that you avoid talking to strangers in those places anyway.

If you find yourself resisting the notion that choice of clothes matters in first impressions, remember that people don't know you, your character, or your credentials in a first encounter. All they have to go by is what you choose to present. To expect others to assume the best about you, a stranger, or to invest time into getting to know you without the foundation of a relationship or encouraging first impression could be seen as irresponsible or entitled.

I want to clarify I in no way insinuate a message about class nor do I support elitism. Any article of clothing or business attire can be as easily and cost effectively purchased at a thrift store, consignment store, charitable agency, or online as shopping for t-shirts or sandals at a conventional store. The impact of seeing someone put effort into their ensemble, however, can leave a priceless and lasting impact on first impressions. You might call this superficial but it's a natural part of "thin-slicing." Further, we tend to feel more confident and purposeful when more dressed up. Greater confidence, in turn, will affect how you present and the interactions you attract.

I chuckle when I think of all the times my mother would overdress when she left the house. She'd usually be in a dress or skirt, sleek colors, and jewelry even if only going to the grocery store or doctor. As silly as this seemed then, I understand now this represented the regard she held for whoever she might encounter along her day. She simply wanted to present most respectably. Not to mention, it takes almost as much time to put on a nicer shirt as it does a t-shirt, to put on slacks or a skirt as it does sweatpants. No judgment here, but if you knew people would respond to you more positively if you dressed differently, would it be worth trying? If you knew more opportunities would present themselves if you chose one outfit over another, would it be worth experimenting? A few other patterns I've noticed, and this is simply my observation not based on any fashion expertise, bold solid colors seem to make a more memorable impression than patterns. Silky, sleek fabrics and lace also tend to leave a more notable impression. In sum, coordinating clothing by color and style and opting for more formal over casual may enhance first impressions and engage more strangers into conversation with you.

I would be remiss not to add that some of the most successful, intelligent people I've met wore t-shirts, the same dark colors, and sandals or tennis shoes every day that I've known them, and that's perfectly ok. Their humility, professional success, and community contributions are unmatched, so I'm not proposing any correlation between attire and goodness, character, or brightness. I simply ask you to consider how different your interactions with strangers might be if you tried different items on for size, literally and figuratively. If you knew that choosing the t-shirt, wrinkled shorts, or flip flops were costing you new connections and giving the impression that you value comfort over presentation, would it matter? While your relaxed vibe can be welcoming, it may not be as memorable and may not be attracting the variety of people you may want to attract.

Chapter 12:
Be Weird

W eird is memorable! Different is memorable. Stand out; just do so tastefully! You're about to think I'm contradicting myself from Chapter 11 on Dress For Success but follow me. Depending on the setting, I propose you welcome aboard some quirks or accessories that make you memorable. Maybe like me, you love to sparkle and wear rhinestones for bling on your fingernails, outfits, jewelry, hair barrettes, or sneakers. Maybe you wear glasses with noticeable, brightly-colored rims that can't be missed. Perhaps you wear stylish hats or sport a different type of accessory that precedes you, or you love a certain sports team and flaunt their emblems on your clothes or bags. Of course, if you're going to a professional or networking event, I encourage you to consider appropriate social norms and embellish cautiously, but you can still incorporate items that represent your personality, even if simply the flair on a tasteful yet eye-catching tie. One of my favorite accents on a man is when he wears playful trouser socks with cartoon characters or bright-

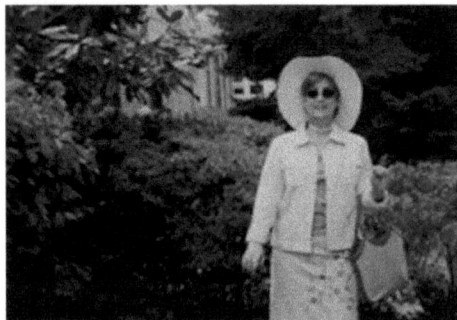

colored shapes alongside an otherwise polished, sophisticated look. You better believe I'll let him know, "Oh my gosh, I LOVE your socks!"

I'm not suggesting you wander into a new environment exaggeratedly accessorized, but don't be afraid to let your personality show in enhancements, like jewelry, wallets, purses, shoes, socks, or scarves. Choose a tasteful item to wear that might make it easier for others to spark a conversation with you. For example, make it natural for others to want to comment, "I love your hat!" Or, "The color of your glasses is so fun!" Or, "Where did you get that tie? I love your flair!" This is about cultivating opportunities that make it easier for others to interact with you. It's about bringing joy and laughter to those around you.

Did you ever watch the MTV reality television show Pickup Artist that aired around 2007? The show was hosted by pickup artist Erik von Markovik who went by the name, "Mystery." I will never forget his eccentric look and accessories. I seem to remember him wearing a hot pink boa out at least once, leopard-print, stripes, some sort of a top hat…I may be making that up, but I can imagine him wearing all of these! He was a very risqué dresser by conventional standards. I recall watching the show wondering how these looks could possibly work for him, and yet, they did. Want to know why they did? Because his boldness and flair engaged others in conversation and intrigue. His quirky enhancements, props if you will, served as talking points. They made conversation fluid, and people bond as they build intrigue and dialogue. Curiosity is powerful in engagement!

A few years ago, I had hot pink and purple highlights that subtly peaked through my otherwise black hair. I've also for years worn bright nail polish colors with sparkles on at least one nail. I was not only taken seriously, but these quirks served as fun talking points when I was out. They're an easy and playful way for people to engage me in conversation and for me to let others know nonverbally that I don't take myself too seriously. How I carry myself matters most. I present with good manners, I speak confidently and intelligently, I present with grace, and it's clear I put effort into coordinating how I dress. I'll be kind to anyone who approaches me, and I'll let them know it was a pleasure speaking with them before I move on. Being kind doesn't mean you stay in conversation for hours. It means you'll treat each person with acknowledgment and manners. It's not uncommon that I'll talk to the person no one else is approaching. I'm quick to open dialogue because I don't fear rejection in a greeting. What would it mean if someone weren't receptive to my kindness in simply opening dialogue? Well, it tells me more about them than it does me. They know nothing about me, but I'd know that at least at that moment in time they did not feel approachable. Let me be clear, they might be warm by nature but at that moment did not present as such, and first impressions are about critical moments, thin-slices of time.

Another way I'm quirky is around numbers. I'm more likely to set my alarm clock to wake me at 5:17 am than at 5:30 am or 5:15 am. The mind tends to recall and retain anomalies more readily than it does more commonly occurring information. It also tends to evoke jokes and laughter. Consider this in making impressions and in inviting people to join you for future events or meetings. Perhaps you might ask, "I'd love to meet again for coffee! What are you doing Friday at 8:23am?"

Did you think it was odd that I chose a somewhat sinister color combination and sharp edges for the cover of this book? I incorporated red for a more eye-catching presence, yet the juxtaposition with black might seem menacing or reminiscent of a horror novel. I thought the marriage of red and black, the yin and yang if you might, could disarm the fear or 'danger' some associate with talking to strangers and welcome the beauty that can be borne in talking to strangers (again, in safe settings and heeding the wiser messages of your intuition).

Another great way to incorporate fun and silliness in new meetings is in commenting on shirts printed with humorous messages. When I see a message I find funny, I simply giggle and say, "I love your shirt," or "Your shirt's hilarious!" I might ask someone where they got their shirt or playfully relate to what's printed on it. Conversations that start in fun can be remarkably memorable. I'll never forget interning at a detention facility in graduate school when a close friend gifted me a black t-shirt with white print, "I make bad boys worse!" I will *never* forget that shirt, and I'll never forget Rebekah for the laughs that shirt brought into my life. Tell me that's not a memorable conversation starter!

How might you find the sweet spot for being uniquely weird without being off-putting? Ask yourself, 'what are my quirks, and are they qualities someone who loves me might find endearing or potentially offensive?' That's usually a good gauge to get you started. If the latter, look deeper. You might also uncover more of your 'endearing quirks' by thinking about unconventional traits that others have complimented you on …which brings us nicely to the next chapter on complimenting others.

If I were to summarize this chapter with a suggestion on how best to be memorably 'weird' in facilitating first impressions, I'd recommend you *be intentional.*

Chapter 13:
The Power of Compliments

*M*any deny the need for validation from others. Many are uncomfortable with praise and compliments. Nevertheless, recognizing and explicitly commenting on what you like or appreciate about others can energize them and increase the frequency of desirable behaviors in them. Doing so is actually self- and other-serving. It is self-serving as it is empowering to notice your impact on the people and environment around you. It's also great to get more of what you like or want if you continue a relationship with that person. Doing so is other-serving as compliments give others feedback on the qualities they emanated that day that were seen and valued. Let's say, for example, you're someone who seldom smiles. Then, you read this book, drive to a coffee shop across town, and try on your new ninja-esque skills by showing off a toothy smile to strangers you come across. Now, imagine three strangers compliment you on your smile, "You have made my day with your smile" or, "You have a great smile!" Are you more or less likely to keep smiling? I'd guess more. Compliments tend to reinforce the engaging traits that draw others near.

My mind naturally wanders to endless qualities to compliment each time I enter a new setting or meet new people. My eyes are immediately drawn to colors, smiles, outfits, or other eye-catching stimuli I'm attracted to. My mind automatically looks for what's appealing, for what I admire, for qualities I appreciate, and I'm quick to comment on these. This is not because I think my opinion is so valuable. It is because my core values include uplifting others and living without regret. My value is to speak my truth and let people I encounter know what I value about them as I embrace authentic relationships and vulnerability, knowing time is promised to no one. I could speculate for weeks on why I am this way. My father always thought loving, tender things about people and didn't hesitate to share with them, though not with the frequency that I do. He seldom spoke a critical word. My mother is not very open around emotional expression. I was not raised around people who praised much, so maybe I've created the reality I would enjoy getting back. Or, perhaps I've been forever molded by extensive years of studying and publishing suicide research since graduate school. I've studied countless examples of the negative and at times life-threatening implications of feeling emotionally *unseen*, and I want to be part of the positive change I want to see in the world. Either way, my complimenting patterns are another trained behavior I've practiced into habit over years. Incidentally, it takes confidence to compliment others. It shows you're not threatened by another's strengths or successes.

In a chapter on complimenting I'd be remiss not to mention too the importance of graciously receiving compliments. Not everyone is comfortable receiving compliments. I encourage you to consider how awkward it feels when you pay someone a compliment and they seem at a loss for what to say, look down uncomfortably, or push away the compliment with some variant of, "Oh no, I'm not." Or consider the person who smugly says, "Thanks," then turns away as if your comment were commonplace or insignificant. Neither is gracious nor welcoming of further exchange. Little about this interaction would leave me wanting more. Instead of minimizing a compliment, look the person in the eyes and say, "I really appreciate that, thank you so much." Feel the empowerment that comes with receiving the compliment and gift you give others in graciously receiving the investment they made in that moment in time with you. Please know I in no way propose that another person's opinion of you gives you value. I'm simply asking that you appreciate others' efforts to see and verbalize the good in you and others. Let's reinforce increased recognition of goodness and kindness in the world around us.

If this were a book on furthering relationships, I'd stress the importance of complimenting at a disproportionately higher rate than criticizing or correcting. Since we're focusing on first impressions, I recommend you simply focus on recognizing and verbalizing positives. Express them all. When I train my business team, I coach them to walk into a room and look sincerely for who and where their eyes are drawn to, then to comment on what they naturally appreciate. Life's too short. If you like someone's tie, say so. If you love the hot pink highlights in someone's hair, say so. If you love those fabulous high heels someone's wearing, say so. If someone has lusciously long eyelashes, say so! If you appreciate the service you received, by all means, say so. You might even help someone learn their endearing quirks by complimenting qualities or manners others might overlook. Simply help make the world a better place.

I would caution you about a few 'no-no's' of complimenting. Avoid comments about physical traits that may be interpreted as sexual in nature. Please don't compliment insincerely. If you don't mean it, don't say it. Inauthentic compliments can land mockingly, which is neither kind nor helpful. Also, in complimenting strangers, express the compliment then either look away or change the subject to avoid lingering eye contact or awkwardness.

One final thought before moving on is to praise and celebrate others' accomplishments. If others share about accomplishments or projects they're proud of, resist the urge to compete for attention by sharing your own. Use these opportunities to let others know you think they're great and that you're interested in learning more about them. Allow them to have the stage.

"Be the change you wish to see in the world."

- Mahatma Ghandi

Chapter 14:
Express Gratitude

*M*any people lump expressions of gratitude in with praise and compliments, possibly because it's become less commonplace in our society to recognize positive contributions. Especially in the workplace and in the context of romantic relationships, people seem increasingly focused on anticipating challenges and parts 'needing repair' instead of highlighting and celebrating what's going well. We've become primed to think about what's *wrong* in hopes of avoiding perceived failure or rejection. This is usually to protect ourselves, systems, and relationships, but doing so can interfere with the very results we want. A heart of gratitude and focus on what's *right* instead permeates to those around us and enriches our relationships.

Gratitude involves directly and clearly expressing thanks for what you appreciate in and about someone or something. It's more than simply saying, "I appreciate you" or "Thanks." It's saying, "I appreciate you for …" and elaborating in a detailed fashion on the specific behaviors, statements, or choices you appreciated. You might even explain how another person's actions positively impact you. Something I regularly say when someone goes out of their way to hold a door open for me, for example, is: "Wow, thank you so much. That is so kind of you." I might even go so far as to let the person know they're a 'wonderful reminder of kindness and chivalry in the world!' Be the person willing to be inconvenienced by taking the extra minute to hold the door open for someone else who's still several steps away. By the way, having a heart of gratitude doesn't stop at people. Motivational author Louise Hay used to wake thanking her bed in the mornings and affirming daily abundance in life. Imagine how doing so impacted the rest of her day or how it might influence yours.

Let others know how they have impacted you or your way of thinking. This is the difference between a superficial thanks and meaningful expression of gratitude. Another example of a sincere and connected expression of gratitude might be, "I so appreciate you for offering to be an editor for my book. You mean the world to me. I know how busy you are, and I feel so cared for by your interest and support of my work." Or, "Thank you so much for taking me to dinner. I feel so loved by your generosity and so enjoy sharing my time with you."

Blanchard and Johnson (1996) in the book *One Minute Manager* reference how effective giving thanks can be in the workplace. They elaborate on how people who feel good about themselves produce good results. The authors specifically recommend "one-minute praisings" as ways to let counterparts know in no uncertain terms what you appreciate about their contributions and expressions. They suggest that a great way to do this is by catching others as they do things well and telling them specifically what you appreciated.

You might wonder how easily you could apply this skill in chance meetings or brief interactions with strangers. Allow me to demonstrate: "Sarah, it has been such a pleasure talking with you. I so appreciate the referrals you recommended today." You could stop there, or if you wish for the possibility of future follow-up, you might add, "I would love to learn more about how I can support you/your business. Would you mind if we connect by phone or e-mail? I would love to stay in touch." See Chapter 18 on the 'After-Impression' to learn more about strategies for fostering ongoing relationships beyond the initial connection. Other examples of expressing gratitude in brief encounters include: "Thank you so much for your suggestion of the French Onion Soup, it was absolutely delicious! One of the best I've had! You clearly have great taste." Or, "I so appreciated your energy today. You are such a friendly face in the room." You might also say, "Thank you so much for spending part of your day with me today. I have enjoyed learning about you."

I'd lose count if I tried to name all of the incredible people and friends I've made over the years as a result of saying something nice to a stranger. Two of my dearest friends I met in public venues. I felt drawn to them in a room, walked up to them, and simply told them so: "You have the most radiant glow/energy about you." Each of these women gave me a huge smile when I first looked their way, letting me know they were open and likely to be kind and welcoming if I introduced myself. The rest is history.

Imagine how different life would feel if you thanked the Universe or your higher power for every inconvenience in your life, assuming each somehow protected you or someone from potential harm or pain? Regardless of how your expressions of gratitude land, I hope you'll feel pride, excitement, and influence in knowing that someone heard words of appreciation because of you. I also hope you celebrate that in sharing gratitude with others, you are modeling dignity, manner, and grace. You are personally making the world a better place. Now *that's* powerful.

Chapter 15:

Welcome Being Wrong

*W*elcome being wrong. Challenge yourself to look for what you might learn from each person you meet along your journey. Watch how others interact. Focus on what you like or admire rather than what you don't. Research has shown that people enjoy associating with people who acknowledge their mistakes and are put off by those who must prove themselves right (Carnegie, 1982). Many are actually more drawn to those with a quiet, inner confidence and humility and to people who don't need to look good or be right. Be comfortable sharing the light, and please don't confuse *quiet* for passive or meek.

Ask yourself how you feel when you prove someone wrong in the interest of proving yourself right? Does it feel good to put another down? I'd argue not. As Carlson (1997) points out in his text *Don't Sweat the Small Stuff, and It's All Small Stuff,* your heart, the compassionate part of you, does not feel better at the expense of another. There is a price to pay for insisting on being right—your inner peace and sometimes the relationship, as resentment rather than appreciation tends to build. Focus on connecting, not correcting. Connecting and uplifting others feels good, especially when the relationship is reciprocal or new. Before correcting others or arguing a point, ask yourself, "What do I want out of this interaction?" Ask, "How important is it for me to feel heard or understood right now?" Or, "What's more important to me? Being right or the relationship?" You'll experience the peace of letting go as you realize not everything must be defined by your terms. You'll also discover the joy of letting others be right when you simply listen and extend appreciation for another's perspective. Others will likely feel less defensive, kinder, and more open toward you as a result. If for some reason they don't, that's okay too. You'll have the inner satisfaction of knowing you've done your part to create a more loving world, and you'll feel more at peace with yourself.

What if you say or do something awkward or off-putting in an interaction? Do you ignore it and pretend it didn't happen? Should you apologize or at least acknowledge it? Many people have an uncomfortable relationship with the words, "I'm sorry." Healthy, appropriately delivered apologies, though, can be healing, uniting, and indicative of integrity. Apologizing is simply letting others know you're sorry they're upset or hurt, not necessarily taking responsibility for the upset. It's also letting others know you care more about the relationship than about being right.

Recovering from a poor first impression involves pausing and reflecting on what went awry and addressing it, if appropriate. Were you late? Did you make a joke before knowing someone's sense of humor, background, or belief system? Once you've reflected, apologize and consider asking for an opportunity to redeem yourself. Seek out the person to whom you owe the apology. Acknowledge what you believe went wrong and how you'll do things differently in the future.

A highly effective way to apologize is to start by saying, "I was wrong, and I'm so sorry." Go on to suggest the corrective action you plan to pursue to repair or re-build trust. If a relationship is to continue, trust must be gained over time. Accept that it may not be immediately given. Be even more prepared to present your best self next time. Arrive early, spend more time listening, and get to know the person's personality and needs before interjecting your own. Not every bad first impression can be made up, but you can stand in integrity knowing you tried nobly (if you did). Please do note, simply saying "Sorry" or "I'm sorry I offended you," or any other variation of a generic apology without a clear indication of understanding what went wrong. Vague apologies generally do not land well and feel insincere to the recipient. And for Pete's sake, never tell someone to "relax" or that they're "too sensitive." The most important part of an effective apology is that you convey a sincere understanding of what went wrong and a reparative plan for preventing similar indiscretions in the future.

Ruiz (2012) suggested in *The Four Agreements* that we refrain from making assumptions and ask for clarification whenever in doubt. He reinforced asking for what we want and being impeccable with our word. In other words, we are to say what we mean and ask for clarity when unsure of others' thoughts, feelings, and needs. These are essential ingredients to happiness in life and healthy, meaningful relationships.

It's natural to fumble and make awkward statements as you start paying more attention to how you present socially as you create your new and improved stranger-loving self. Don't hesitate to apologize and accept responsibility if you make comments that are poorly timed or delivered. If, for example, you make a joke that is not well-received, say something like, "I apologize, I shouldn't have made that joke. Sometimes my nerves get the better of me. Can we start over?" or some alternative of that. I would especially recommend this if you make potentially sexist, racist, or other offensive joke or comment against subgroups of people or belief systems. Some make jokes in wanting to relate to others, others in wanting to diffuse their own discomfort in new situations. Especially in new affiliations where you don't know others' values and belief systems, this is risky. I'd recommend you ask yourself if your comfort is worth the risk of damaging others' feelings. Off-color humor can sever any possibility of a future relationship.

I would be remiss not to elaborate on sarcasm while we discuss scenarios that may warrant an apology. Many people use sarcasm as a vehicle for delivering humor, defending their use of sarcasm as an attractive trait representing intelligence and wit. I see sarcasm very differently. Sarcasm is defined by various online sources as the *'use of irony to mock or convey contempt.'* Merriam-Webster Dictionary defines sarcasm as "sharp and often satirical or ironic utterance *designed to cut or give pain;* satirical wit that has the effect of *bitter, caustic, and often ironic language* that is *usually directed against an individual.* Would you still see sarcasm as an attractive quality as defined here? I don't.

Sarcasm seldom lands in a way that fosters positive relationship-building and can be highly damaging to the foundation of relationships over time. Sarcasm is often a passive-aggressive way of communicating envy or resentment of some quality or behavior in another person. Sarcasm over time can deepen insecurities and tension in relationships, especially when calling attention to qualities that are problematic in a partnership. Some people become defensive when their sarcasm isn't well-received and invalidate others' feelings by accusing them of being "too sensitive." Instead, offer an apology: "I apologize, I realize my sarcasm can be off-putting at times," then redirect the conversation to a more positive topic Or, you might ask a question to show interest in the other person. If the other person needs to talk about their reactions to your sarcasm and feel heard, please let them.

Finally, while I suggested avoiding expectations, I do see value in expecting inconvenience everywhere you go. View meeting strangers as an adventure. Adventures are meant to have an element of surprise, and we can't have surprises without allowing for the unexpected. Expect awkward silences. Expect others to relate in ways you don't resonate with. Resist the urge to correct them or tell them you disagree, unless necessary. I don't propose you abandon yourself, your values, or your needs to make others comfortable. I do ask that you avoid wounding or embarrassing others as you honor yourself, your preferences, and your boundaries. Practice healthy, respectful, and kind ways to excuse yourself from interactions. Thank whoever you're talking to for their time, and politely excuse yourself to the bathroom or next conversation you're looking forward to discovering.

Chapter 16:
Bring the Power

*A*re you aware of your power? We all have it. But, do you express it and let it out? That's how you'll know your impact. Did you know there are certain postures, words, and colors associated with power? Let's talk first about colors. If you google the *color red as a power color*, you'll find that red is described as the color of *fire and blood*, associated with *energy, war, danger, strength, power, determination, passion, desire, and love*! Tell me those aren't powerful words! Red is also cited by google as a highly emotionally intense color that "enhances human metabolism, increases respiration rate, and raises blood pressure." This color actually impacts our bodily functions!

Connecting and impression-making are all about standing out as memorable. This doesn't mean being loud or obnoxious but simply being noticed and leaving an emotional impact. Wearing red or a similarly bright, vibrant color is an easy way to do this. Wearing bold colors also leads to feeling bolder and more confident. It's no coincidence that the cover of this book is emblazoned in red. 'Emblazoned,' how's that for a power word? Would you notice a red book on a coffee table or bookshelf? I would. Do be careful, wearing a vibrant color doesn't guarantee *positive* interactions and can even hurt your impression if you make an otherwise negative impression. Since reds and bright colors stand out in a crowd, you're remembered for whatever you present. If you neglect the positive connecting behaviors in this book, you are more likely to be remembered but for the less attractive behaviors you present, so use caution.

How about power through words? Power words are defined differently depending on context. If writing a resume, power words are considered active tense words that tend to carry an emotional charge, such as 'excelled, innovated, pioneered, or generated.' If you used these in initial meetings, though, you might outcast yourself. I believe power words for talking to strangers and initial impressions are words demonstrating polish and manner that have become less commonplace over passing generations. When used, they tend to leave a positive emotional impact. Examples of phrases I was raised to use in extending social graces include, "It is my pleasure," "The pleasure is mine," "It's my honor to meet you," "I so appreciate you/your time/your care," "Your customer service is exceptional, thank you," "I'm humbled," "My sincerest thanks," "May I...," "Respectfully," "I can't thank you enough." Other power words that flow well in conversation include expressions that evoke action or movement such as, "Let's move forward" instead of "Let's move to." Words can be used to add emphasis and build others up, or they can have the opposite effect. Let's be a part of the movement that builds up.

I was in Cabo two weeks before I started writing this book, and a lovely friend I made on the trip joined me for dinner. The server greeted us, "Good evening, ladies. It is my sincere honor to be at your service this evening." My friend and I melted. She glowed and commented on how seldom people talk this way in today's world. I couldn't agree with her more. His manner left us feeling like we were the only table that mattered at that moment. It didn't matter to us that he was likely saying that to every other table there. A memorable barista in town welcomes patrons by asking, "How can I make your day better today?" Finally, as I was finalizing this book over lunch, my server said in closing, "You are such a pleasure to serve. Come back and see me." You better believe I will! Power words move us and inspire action.

As for power posture, search TED Talks on the Superman and Superwoman poses. They direct you to stand up tall (if physically able to), throw your arms up and out, and feel the power of the stance. Taking up space with these postures is said to fuel confidence and can be especially helpful in calming nerves before important moments, events, or going on stage. The videos are worth the online search and the poses worth trying.

There are so many powerful ways to greet people and comparably powerful ways to exit new meetings. I hope by now you've equated *powerful* to *memorable*. There is quite a difference between saying: "Hi, I'm Elicia" versus "Good evening, I'm Elicia! It's an honor to meet you. Thank you so much for having me." It's one thing to say "Thanks, bye" versus "Thank you so much for having me. Your event was lovely. I met so many incredible people. You clearly attract wonderful people into your sphere. I hope to see you again." Which version of *you* do you want to leave behind?

Chapter 17:
Location, Location, Location

hy do I repeat myself here? I cannot stress enough how critical physical space is in establishing connections. How you position yourself in a room matters almost as much in talking to strangers as location matters in real estate! Where you sit or stand directly impacts how accessible you are in meeting strangers. You may be exuding the friendliest, warmest, most approachable energy in a room, but if you're not readily accessible, you make it harder for others to physically reach you. Proximity and access facilitate engagement. Imagine wanting to speak to someone but having to wade through a crowd of people and furniture in a large auditorium to get there. It's much more difficult to initiate a conversation with someone when obstacles and distance must be overcome to do so. That leaves ample time for insecurities to take over.

What does addressing location look like when interacting with strangers? Well, you'll rarely see me seated at a private table if a community table is available. If I'm to choose between one open seat at a community table or a table to myself, I'm choosing the community seat, no matter who else is sitting there. By my philosophy, every chance meeting has a grander purpose we may not know for years to come. I welcome and make space for each one.

I wrote this chapter sitting at a coffee bar at a new local coffee house. Almost every table was open when I got here, and I intentionally chose a seat at the end of the bar. Doing so allowed me to interact with those who'd sit next to me as well as passersby awaiting their drinks at the side of the bar. I welcome whoever is destined along my path and look up often to engage with eye contact. I banter with proximal bystanders when I think of something to banter about. Then, I get back to business. The interactions don't last long. They're simply small moments in time I co-create with nearby friendly others. Each of these momentary interactions allows for a meaningful connection, short-lived or otherwise. Who gives it meaning? I do.

Another way I incorporate space when out is by moving fluidly through a crowd. When at an event, I move about. I'm open and curious about what's around each corner and assume any encounter may be memorable. This fluidity sends the message that I'm taking in the experience and not married to a certain place or person, which again welcomes others to engage as I proceed along my adventure.

Speaking of adventure, I mentioned earlier withholding expectations as much as possible. We discussed how having expectations can result in missing fabulous moments that fall outside of the realm of what we're looking for. I do, however, encourage you to *expect* to find 'adventures.' Pursue events with an attitude of curiosity. Adventures implicitly engage an element of curiosity whereas expectations tend to mute curiosity. When pursuing events with this affinity for finding adventure, you're more likely to be excited and open to unexpected moments. You're also more likely to be met with an endearing element of child-like awe.

Let's revisit the caution about positioning around hurdles. Would someone interested in talking with you have to go around tables, chairs, and/or groups of people to reach you for conversation? Are you situated in a crowd of people another person might have to insert themselves into to talk with you? If so, consider that many people find walking over to initiate a conversation intimidating to begin with and to do so by having to interrupt a multi-person conversation is even more daunting. Some people think going out in groups makes them appear more friendly, fun, and open, thereby attracting more connections. I believe the opposite to be true. I find that I am far more frequently approached when out alone than when out in a group that someone would have to interrupt to speak with me.

Speaking of location, consider everything around you a prop in creating memories. If you're at the grocery store and want to talk to someone who's standing by the oranges, walk over and comment on the wonderful aura of citrus in a fun, banter-like way: "These oranges smell so great! You'd think we were in Florida." If at a concert, ask what someone's go-to item is at the food stand you're in line for. Lean in, be playful about it, then lean back. If at a clothing store, let a person you pass know which color of the item they're browsing you think would most complement them: "I think the red would look great on you!" Then, keep walking! You definitely don't want to create memories by hovering and making it awkward. If the person you approach doesn't comment, that's ok. Move on, proud that you tried and remind yourself: "Maybe they're having a bad day, or maybe they didn't hear me." Repeating yourself might, however, make it awkward so try again elsewhere.

So, we talked about positioning in a room. How about the positioning of your body in place? Do you have your back to the person you'd like to speak to or to the crowd at an event? Have you closed yourself off to others behind you, making it more awkward for them to approach you? What's the path someone would have to take to speak with you? Would they have to uncomfortably meander around your group to introduce themselves? Keep moving and intermingle moments of talking to people with moments when you're curiously walking about the room alone, open and comfortably available for the start of the next conversation. Consider keeping your phone in your pocket or otherwise out of sight as it is a deterrent to positive engagement.

There are a few common mistakes I see people make at events. For starters, please avoid hovering in doorways or at the registration table. You end up blocking the flow of movement in and out of the room and may appear to have little regard for others around you. Further, avoid targeting one or two people at an event you think you *must* talk to at the expense of meeting others. Many people make assumptions about their compatibility with certain people over others. This idolization inappropriately fixates them and can end up disappointing, interfering with a potentially more positive experience with others. You'll only know true compatibility over time, repeated exposure, and by asking good questions to build a relationship over time, so broaden your reach.

In short, I recommend that you *be easy!* Obviously, I don't mean *that* kind of easy. Remove as many barriers as you can to make it easier for new connections to take flight. Fears, insecurities, and social strengths of others are not within your control but maneuvering yourself, your body, and where you stand (or sit) in space are. Doing so strategically is an invaluable way of creating a safe environment for new connections to thrive.

Chapter 18:

'After' Impressions: Meet Me Inside

*Y*our first gift is in the connection. Congratulations! If you've made it this far, you've learned how to establish memorable connections and refine the art of first impressions. Relationships happen in the follow-up. I'm sure you've heard the saying, "the fortune's in the follow-up." Relationships are not always easy to manage. I can't tell you how often I've established a strong connection with an unforgettable stranger then failed to follow-up for any host of excuses from being busy, forgetful, waiting so long that it got awkward...you name it. I've also met great people who seemed blown away by me in an initial meeting who failed to effectively follow-up. Why do we do this? Why do we invest our time and energy into people, forge strong initial connections, build memorable moments, then miss the boat on cultivating a genuine relationship? Honestly, I'm not concerned with the why because that simply welcomes excuses. Let's just stop and *be better*.

For years I've been known as a "connector" in the communities I serve, from psychology to skincare. All this means is when I meet someone looking for a particular something and I knew another person who could provide it, I excitedly say, "I know someone you might want to meet!" Or, "I'd love to connect you with my colleague [name]. I think the two of you would have a lot to talk about. May I put you in touch?" Or simply, "I'd love to learn more about you. May I get your email/phone number?" Seldom will someone say "No, you may not have a way to ever reach me again. I will be riding off into the sunset today, never to be reached again, but I fancied getting to know you." Sorry, I digress. I do recommend you follow-up *immediately* after meeting with a note reminding you both of where, how, and when you met: "Hi [insert name here]! It was great meeting you at charity event this weekend! I look forward to reconnecting!" This also allows you both to share responsibility in establishing a genuine relationship after meeting if there is to be one. Using complete sentences and power words is a good rule of thumb when initiating follow-up. Please do not text "what's up" or "hey" to new contacts. Including a question in your message is a great way to get conversation flowing. A phone call is even more impressive, although some people in today's world have an estranged relationship with phone calls.

Aziz Ansari (2015) in *Modern Romance* describes how differently romance and relationships were cultivated in generations past. Courtship and accessibility to meeting partners were very different then, yet some principles he identified can still be used today in building connections of any kind, from professional to personal. Ansari describes how attraction and chemistry develop as common experiences are shared, inside jokes are developed, and familiarity builds over successive meetings. This is no different in fostering relationships beyond chance encounters, whether for personal or professional pursuits.

I've secured great joy over years of connecting people. It's energizing to unite people who may help one another create, whether they're creating business plans, events, or shared life memories. Doing so also affords me the gift of seeing a person's integrity and character. Do the people I connect show gratitude or entitlement in the connection? Do they show manners in follow-up? Do they present as reliable? It is in the 'after' impression that it becomes clear whether a first impression is upheld. If you keep in touch with people you've met, they begin to learn more about you, and you about them. It is then that you'll learn if your core values are in alignment.

As someone who takes joy in connecting others, I have little expectation of return. With that said, I advocate for self-respect and boundaries. Imagine month after month, year after year you repeatedly connected the same individuals to resources and referrals, yet they seldom reciprocate with shared opportunities, referrals, or gratitude? I have found this to be a gauge of someone's integrity, investment, and authenticity in a shared relationship. Rules of reciprocity would suggest that people respond in kind to how they are treated, so look for ways to support others and take note of whether they extend gratitude and support to you. If connections do not return loyalty over time, it's natural to begin questioning the relationship and redirect attention elsewhere. Until given reason not to, share generosity of time, resources, connections, and spirit without overextending yourself. Know what you're willing to give open-heartedly with no expectation of return. Know your personal limits to ensure you're not taken advantage of. Don't keep score but notice if your kindness is periodically returned. Think of it this way; if a person doesn't value reciprocity with you, how confident are you that they'll treat your contacts and friends with integrity and loyalty? Would you want to entrust people you care about to someone with seemingly self-serving motives and interests?

When following up, be sincere in sharing what you appreciated about the first meeting. Speak directly, kindly, and without an agenda. Even if you initially spoke about work, *show interest in the person before the business*. Get to know one another, what you stand for, and what you're passionate about. Show your reliability and care for relationships and principles. If you offered to follow-up with resources or business-specific information, do so but welcome a human connection *first*. Comment on something your connections shared with you when you first met. Ask how the people and activities that mattered most to them have been in the days that have passed. This will go much further than any indication of business competence you might reflect in a credential or financial portfolio. Show modesty and humanize your connections. Show genuine kindness and care for a person's condition. As Teddy Roosevelt said, *"Nobody cares how much you know until they know how much you care."* Find something in the other person to care about. Don't *pretend* to care; genuinely care and show it.

Chapter 19:
Keeping It Personal
Through Technology

*J*ust as I was wrapping up the book, a colleague reminded me to include tips on using technology for nurturing relationships beyond initial connections. Nothing has taught me more about how to do this effectively and authentically than managing a global online anti-aging skincare business. Below, you'll find some quick and easy tips for using technology to track, cultivate, and deepen relationships.

Create a virtual business card (vCard) on your cell phone. This means adding a new contact to your phone's contact address book with your *own* contact information. Include your name, phone number, e-mail address, and website if you have one. Include a photo or logo you'd like to be remembered by to personalize the contact download. Save this vCard to your cell phone home screen so it's quick and easy to get to. When you meet people you feel chemistry with (personal or professional), let them know: "I've really enjoyed meeting you. Would you mind if I text you my phone number so we can reconnect or collaborate on a future project?" Or, perhaps you might invite them to an upcoming event and say, "I have several folks I'd love to connect you to. Would it be alright to send you a text, so we have one another's information?" Most people will say yes. You'll then click on your personalized vCard, click on the dots that usually appear in the top corner of the contact, then select *Share* to share your contact information with them. Enter their phone number along with a brief message. Let them know your vCard can be saved directly into their phone's address book to be later found among their contacts. I'd recommend including in the text a message letting them know what a pleasure it was meeting them and mentioning where or how you met. The easier you make it for others to remember you, the more likely the connection is to grow. No one wants to admit they don't remember how they met you, so help them save face. And heck, as you become a stranger magnet, you'll need a way to keep all your new friends straight!

Another important consideration is electronic etiquette. It's not unusual nowadays for people to use shortcuts when communicating electronically and yet it is just as important, if not moreso, to come across as professional, conscientious, detail-oriented, and polished when relying on a virtual impression. Avoid abbreviations or acronyms, one-word messages, missed capitalization or punctuation, slang, and other shortcuts when communicating via text or email at least for the first few messages when establishing credibility. More polished communication is especially important if following up for professional reasons and in the interest of optimizing first impressions. Once a relationship is established, this is less important as communication may become more relaxed and congenial and shared jokes are established.

It's great practice to ask how the people you're meeting prefer to communicate. In today's digital age, some people prefer text messages or emails, and some still prefer phone calls. I prefer communicating by Voxer, which is a walkie talkie app that allows an exchange of real-time voice messages. I don't enjoy communication by text unless in the context of business or romantic partnership for brief exchanges. I much prefer to hear the inflection in someone's voice.

The context of a relationship is important to consider in avoiding absolutes around technology. For example, if I'm interested in someone's care, wisdom, or business, I would assume responsibility for communicating in their preferred medium. Likewise, I would hope if someone values a relationship with me, personal or professional, and especially if they seek something from me, that they would show interest in communicating with me in ways that I can most easily uphold. The principle of reciprocity reminds us to consider mutual gratification in relationships.

A final suggestion when wanting to establish and maintain longer-term relationships is to invite people as friends and contacts on social media platforms and to appropriately brand yourself there in a diversified fashion. Have your social media represent the whole of you. Show your personality. Show who and how you are so people added there see not only the professional you but the *you* as a unique person. My Facebook page represents my passion for sharing inspiration, humor, friends, resilience, charity, and travel. I share invitations to events I host, charity events I support, and posts for my skincare business representing our team and products. Additionally, I try to highlight my personality and uplift as often as I can. I am proud to be known for all of these sides and brand myself as such. The biggest compliment I get is when someone meets me in real life having primarily known me from social media and says I'm as authentic in person as I seem online.

The overall theme of using media is to allow it to facilitate communication with a greater number of people more seamlessly and without having it detract from the personal connection. Comment on others' pages and posts in appropriate yet meaningful and positive ways. Please leave any personal matters or opinions off the public platforms.

Reach out to your contacts one-on-one, and get to know people as people. See how you can support them before you turn to them to support a cause of yours. Let them know they're unforgettable for something that in no way benefits you. That is the secret to fostering powerful connections that persist beyond chance encounters.

How would you like to be remembered?

Chapter 20:
Until We Meet Again

*I*n closing, I would love to leave you with the overarching message that the best connections are borne simply in bringing out the best in others. Make it your goal to help everyone you meet feel special for that moment in time. Be that person others are glad to have met for no reason other than to make the world a brighter, more enjoyable place.

People want to be around uplifting people. Memorable first impressions are about disarming others with your personality and care for the human spirit. If you help others feel more comfortable around you, they are more likely to show you more of their *true best selves*. That is where real connection and genuine relationships begin to form. Beyond that, I've also found across countless chance encounters with strangers, I've had a heck of a lot more fun in life! If I saw those strangers again in any capacity, that was icing on the cake. If I didn't want to see them again, brief interactions in time were the quickest way to know that our energies were misaligned, and that's ok! I've lived without regret.

Because of the chances I've taken to show up as the person I've outlined in this book, I've shared more giggles in life, I've established incredible memories, and I've felt repeatedly blessed to have crossed paths with unforgettable people, whether for moments in time, business relationships, or years of friendship.

I appreciate you taking the time to read my thoughts. I'm humbled by your support and hope you're able to utilize the tools here to develop new connections and deepen your relationships.

May the end of this book be your new beginning...

*"People come into your life for a **reason**, a **season** or a **lifetime**." – Unknown*

Please, treat each honorably...

References

Ansari, A., & Klinenberg, E. (2015). *Modern Romance*. NY: Penguin Press.

Bianco, M. W. (1975). *The Velveteen Rabbit: or, how toys become real*. New York: N.Y.: Avon Books.

Blanchard, K., & Johnson, S. (1982). *The One-Minute Manager*. NY, NY: Blanchard Family.

Carlson, R. (1997). *Don't Sweat the Small Stuff—And It's All Small Stuff: Simple ways to keep the little things from taking over your life*. New York: Hyperion.

Carnegie, D. (1982). *How to Win Friends & Influence People*. First Pocket Books: NY, NY.

Casey, K. (2003). *Fearless Relationships: Simple rules for lifelong contentment*. MN: Hazelden Publishing.

Chabris, C., & Simons, D. (2009). *The Invisible Gorilla: How are intuitions deceive us*. NY, NY: Random House, Inc.

Gladwell, M. (2005). *Blink: The Power of thinking without thinking*. New York: Little, Brown, and Co.

Gladwell, M. (2002). *Tipping Point*. Boston, MA: First Back Bay Publishing.

Kabat-Zinn, J. (1994). *Wherever You Go, There You Are: Mindfulness meditation in everyday life*. New York: Hyperion.

Merriam-Webster.com. Merriam-Webster, 2019. Web. 4 October 19.

Nichols, M. P. (1995). *The Lost Art of Listening: How learning to listen can improve relationships.* New York: Guilford Press.

Ruiz, D. M. (2012). *The Four Agreements: A practical guide to personal freedom.* *San Rafael,* CA: Amber-Allen Publishing, Inc.

Ryan, M. J. (2005). *The Happiness Makeover: How to teach yourself to be happy and enjoy every day.* Random House Crown Publishing: Harmony Books.

Tarrant, J. (2004). *Bring Me the Rhinoceros & Other Zen Koans To Bring You Joy.* NY: Harmony Books.

Acknowledgments

A huge debt of gratitude goes to my dear friend and colleague, Steve W., who has helped me countless times both in sharing wisdoms around personal and work relationships and as an advocate in the mental health advocacy world. It was Steve's stroke of genius that ignited the writing of this book. Thanks for always forcing me to take an honest look at myself, for better or worse. Another huge thanks to Patrick Ready for inspiring the title for this book. Pat's quick wit, humor, and support are unmatched! The world needs many more like you in it!

I couldn't have felt as confident sharing this book without the support and input of dear friends Diana Gettman Flores and Jeremy Ward. Diana and Jeremy, I am grateful for your gracious and selfless willingness to provide feedback on the book before it went public. You are both examples of kindness and purity of heart, and I'm blessed to have attracted you both into my world. Diana, the countless times you read and re-read this text is simply touching. Your friendship, patience, and support are priceless. Jim Shaw, you sir are a model of the success that comes from applying the skills laid out herein. You exemplify the random kindness the world has to offer. From day one, you've met my kindness with kindness, my personality with yours, and you've enthusiastically volunteered yourself to be of service when you had nothing to gain for it. Your cheerleading and confidence in me through helping to revise this book and your countless examples of how you could relate to the text have made this venture exciting and fun! You are sincerely an example of what I lay out in this book -- ways to make others around you feel like a million bucks for no reason other than to make a completely unselfish, positive impact on the world around you. I think you'd be first in line to buy beach-front property in the desert if I were selling it simply because you're that incredible of a supporter!

Bill Morgan and John Buchholz of SCORE for small business development, you gentlemen have been among my biggest cheerleaders. You've helped me develop my skill and confidence as an entrepreneur. You challenge me to think outside of my comfort zone, and you offer support every step of the way. A special note of thanks too to my friend and colleague, fellow psychologist Dr. Frederick Wechsler. Fred was one of the first people I published with and lit the author's fire up under me. I thank you! Likewise, Stephanie Scott-Snyder, you are also a source of inspiration to me as the trailblazer of authors in my life. Thank you for sharing your publishing wisdoms. Finally, Erica Van Der Heyden, thank you for being an incredible colleague and support in countless ways. I always appreciate your extra set of eyes and guidance.

I couldn't have made it through painful years of graduate school and a busy career without the tireless and self-less love of my mother who stores delicious Persian meals in my freezer for the days when I run myself ragged and too tired to cook and who checks on her grand-pup when I'm gone long hours, forever seeking work-life balance. I also wouldn't be here had she not been wise enough to choose my father as her partner in life. I don't know where I'd be without the love and support they instilled in me growing up and still today. I'd be remiss not to mention my pup-child Kaylex for the countless hours she has spent on my lap as I've written, read, and brainstormed along my journey to authorship. Kaylie, you unquestionably give a new definition to the charm of a chihuahua and to the loyalty of family.

I don't know where I'd be without the partnership, friendship, and love of my friend and Rodan + Fields business partner, Brooke Hosman-Fremouw. Brooke, you've carried on my father's torch in the most unexpected ways. You naturally emanate the grace, humility, patience, and unconditional love my father upheld. You remind me every day of the standard I want to live up to. You've accepted me when I didn't accept myself. You've helped ignite my light when it was flickering out. You've helped me identify and understand my faith, guided me in prayer and spiritual fulfillment, and never judged me along the way no matter how deeply I questioned myself. You're a constant reminder to show compassion even when it is the hardest choice. You give generously, love honorably, and live proudly. You're an incredible mother, wife, and friend. I am beyond humbled to call you a friend and role model as you minister to and support children around the world. You're also an incredible and selfless sidekick in our business which has taught me more about relationships and life than I could ever have imagined.

I could go on and on naming dear friends Beth Mehin, Sarah Burgamy, Saneyee Karve, Melissa Wasie, Suzanne Coyne, Marveasha Primonato, Jessi Brogan, Gina Monteiro, Sofia Galinski, Leigh Johnson Miller, Catie Pettit, and Candace Schacherbauer among others who've borne witness to my life, holding space while I speak aloud my heart's aches and desires. You've each loved me through struggles and successes. You've challenged me to look deeper, push further, and see myself and others through life-altering lenses. Heck, some of you love me the hardest on my worst days for no identifiable reason, and *that* is priceless. I'm blessed to be surrounded by so many who remind me regularly of my contributions. You've respected me, challenged me, and empowered me when I've questioned my impact, and you've encouraged me as I, sometimes clumsily, create my authentic life. I can only hope I do half of that for each of you. I love you all and am grateful for your light and wisdom in my life.

About the Author

*D*r. Nademin is a board certified psychologist in behavioral and cognitive psychology. She works full-time as a home-based primary care psychologist for older, medically-compromised veterans. She maintains a small part-time private practice, and lectures annually on professionalism, communication, behavioral medicine, and diversity to medical students. She has been involved in standard-setting and curriculum development for communication, interpersonal skills, and behavioral medicine for students of osteopathic medicine. She has held multiple leadership roles in the Arizona Psychological Association and has long overseen diversity advocacy efforts in her community. Dr. Nademin also serves as the Arizona Early Career Psychologist Ambassador to the American Board of Professional Psychology.

In addition to her work in mental health, Dr. Nademin shines her entrepreneurial spirit as a Rodan + Fields Independent Consultant. As a business owner, she most enjoys watching people dream differently as they grow in confidence, communication, and leadership skills. She has explored entrepreneurial strengths in unique and unexpected ways. She loves watching people feel more in control of the aging process, but more importantly, she is energized by empowering others to lead, inspire, and impact lives through the teams they serve. In her free time, Dr. Nademin spends time with her mother, friends, and dog Kaylie. She most enjoys traveling and watching people share their gifts and talents, from breakdancing to stand-up comedy and spoken word. She especially enjoys volunteering with charity events where she delights in meeting others who share a passion for giving.

In her respective roles, Dr. Nademin gets great fulfillment in helping others build confidence, relationship skills, and community. She promotes diversification, and her business inspires her daily to serve others on a global platform. If interested in learning more about her, please go to her website: www.4ANewYou2.com. If interested in supporting her in business, joining her team, or donating towards the purchase of skincare self-care baskets for charity, please e-mail her at elician@gmail.com or see the Charity Sponsors page of her website. She is also always excited to welcome motivated, caring members aboard her team and into her world, so message her if looking for a new opportunity!

www.ingramcontent.com/pod-product-compliance
Lightning Source LLC
Chambersburg PA
CBHW072148020426
42334CB00018B/1920